MANAGEMENT ENGLISH

COURSE BOOK

K. E. Rowlands

HODDER AND STOUGHTON
LONDON SYDNEY AUCKLAND TORONTO

British Library Cataloguing in Publication Data
Rowlands, K E
   Management English: course book
    1. English language—Text-books for foreigners
    2. English language—Business English
   I. Title
   651.7'4   PE1128

ISBN 0 340 22844 X

Second impression 1980
Copyright © K. E. Rowlands 1979

All rights reserved. No part of this publication may be reproduced or transmitted in any form or by any means, electronic or mechanical, including photocopy, recording, or any information storage and retrieval system, without permission in writing from the publisher.

Printed in Great Britain for Hodder and Stoughton Educational, a division of Hodder and Stoughton Ltd, Mill Road, Dunton Green, Sevenoaks, Kent, by Fakenham Press Limited, Fakenham, Norfolk.

Contents

	Foreword	v
	Introduction	vii
1	The First Day	1
2	In Mr Green's Office	5
3	First Assignments	9
4	David Asks Some Questions	13
5	David Gets Down To Work	18
6	Lunch In The Canteen	22
7	Advertising a New Product	27
8	Selling and Marketing	31
9	The Personnel Manager	35
10	Review of the Week	39
11	The Draft Brochure	44
12	Some Aspects of Selling and Marketing	49
13	The Product Evaluation Meeting—One	53
14	The Product Evaluation Meeting—Two	57
15	Cost-Effectiveness in Business	62
16	The Product Manager is Appointed	66
17	A Visit to the Works—One	70
18	A Visit to the Works—Two	75
19	The Sales Convention—One	80
20	The Sales Convention—Two	84
21	A Tour of the Offices	89
22	Training Opportunities	92
23	More Preparations for the Convention	96
24	At the Castle Hotel	99
25	After the Convention	102
26	The Trade Fair—One	108
27	The Trade Fair—Two	111
28	An Overseas Visitor	114
29	A Business Lunch	117
30	Urgent Discussions	120
31	The Board Meeting	126
32	Consultations	131
33	Negotiations	134

34	The Secretary's Department—One	137
35	The Secretary's Department—Two	140
36	The Draft Agreement	146
37	Insurance	149
38	The Accounts Department	152
39	A Trip Abroad	155
40	Spot-21 Is Launched	158
	Grammar Notes	161

Foreword

In writing Management English I have tried to satisfy four main criteria: first, that it should be adult in concept; second, linguistically balanced to bridge the gap between lower and higher intermediate; third, relevant in content to the needs of the target group, and fourth, that it should help the transition from controlled to free use of the language. As a teacher of languages to business people I am privileged to meet some exceptionally intelligent and able men and women. In one respect only can I safely assume that my knowledge is superior to theirs. In a number of others they are at least my equal; many are my superior. I have always found that even the least linguistically gifted respond well to material suited to their general intellectual level, and perform far better when the topic is relevant, authentic and stimulating than when it is banal and artificially presented. I believe there is no excuse for putting into a student's mouth utterances for which there is little practical use, merely to exercise a grammatical structure. Far better is it, having taught the basic structures—and Management English requires a good foundation in the essential grammar—to demonstrate through natural use of the language how those structures are manipulated in order to communicate.

K.E.R. October 1977.

Introduction

1 Target Group

The course is intended to meet the needs of people at all levels of management who find it necessary or desirable to improve their English for business. It covers a wide selection of the situations and problems with which management has to deal, and the material is designed to give students extensive practice in the use of English for the functions of management. The emphasis is on oral communication and aural comprehension, but written exercises and practice in reading comprehension are also included.

2 Course Level

Of the three generally accepted levels of language learning (elementary, intermediate and advanced), intermediate covers the broadest spread of ability. Many students whose aural comprehension and oral performance are low as the result of lack of exposure to the spoken language have nevertheless a high level of reading comprehension. To overcome this problem, the material for active exploitation begins simply and becomes increasingly more difficult, while a selection of more advanced material is simultaneously available from the outset. The course can thus proceed at varying levels within the intermediate range, depending on the needs and abilities of the students.

3 Course Material

The course comprises a Course Book, an Activities Book and cassettes/tapes.

a) *Course Book*

This contains 40 episodes in the life of Discovery Engineering Ltd, a fictitious company located in Birmingham. Linguistically, the material falls roughly into three parts:

Episodes 1–10 A revision section in which the most important grammatical structures and simple everyday functions are introduced and exercised by means of simple dialogues and activities.

Episodes 11–20 Work on the first section is consolidated with the introduction of additional structures and more advanced functions.

Episodes 21–40 The most advanced part of the course, when students are exposed to idiomatic English at normal speed (including some regional accents) and are required to carry out activities calling for a range of functions. (*Note:* Since students with limited time to spare for full-time study [see note 4— Presentation] may elect to begin the course at this point, Episodes 21 and 22 are comparatively easy.)

Each Episode opens with an introduction followed by a dialogue, lesson notes and comprehension questions. Episodes 1–20 also include drills for use in class or laboratory and there are further drills with Episodes 25, 30 and 35. A set of grammatical notes, keyed to the Episodes, is given at the end of the book for reference.

b) *Activities Book*

This contains 36 Units, of which Units 1–35 are linked to Episodes 1–35 of the Course Book. They are organized on a functional basis; each unit opens with a description of one or more functions, gives examples and suggests techniques for exploiting them. The students are then presented with various suggestions for activities in which the functional techniques can be practised and extended. Unit 36 is a 'project' in which the students consider alternative solutions to the problems of an expanding company which is outgrowing its existing premises. Additional material for reading comprehension, group discussion and written exercises is also included; this consists of specially written articles, extracts from previous publications, advertisements and publicity material, and a selection of plans, organigrams, diagrams, etc., of which a few are fictitious but all are authentic and many are actual.

4 Presentation

a) *General*

Although the course is designed to fit into an intensive, four-week programme of two lessons a day, five days a week, it is accepted that by no means all students using it will follow such a programme. Although all the Episodes are linked by characters and events, the course is sufficiently flexible to allow some of them to be omitted without loss of continuity, and in practice—because of divergent interests— the value of individual episodes will vary from one group to another. The same is true of the material in the Activities Book.

b) *Presenting the Episodes*

This is, of course, a matter for the individual teacher to decide, but it is suggested that each episode be introduced in the classroom, firstly by asking the students to listen to it without the text and then allowing them to read it aloud. The relevant grammar and vocabulary can be studied as necessary and pronunciation errors identified and dealt with. The drills are then considered, and it is important that the students fully understand the purpose of each drill before going into the language laboratory. The principal aim of the drills is to improve fluency, accent, rhythm and intonation; most of them are short and simple to grasp, and none of them requires the student to repeat unnatural phrases merely to exercise points of grammar. The repetition drills (Drill A in each set) are particularly valuable in developing a sense of the rhythm of the language and in improving fluency; beginning with the end of the utterance, the student gradually works backwards, adding a few words at a time until he is speaking the complete phrase or sentence while maintaining the basic rhythm throughout.

Students who have never used a language laboratory before do not always appreciate its possibilities and may tend to work through the exercises once, listen to their recordings and then sit back under the impression that they have done all that is required of them. They must, in their own interests, be made aware of the opportunity the laboratory provides for self-correction. Many of the most persistent pronunciation errors are due, not to a lack of interest or effort on the student's part, but rather to a lack of perception of the true sound he is trying to reproduce. To become aware of the actual 'target sound' by developing the listening faculty is an essential step in rectifying the error.

c) *The Comprehension Questions*

It is envisaged that these will form the final part of the lesson; they are intended to provide feedback for the teacher and to consolidate the factual and linguistic content of the Episode before moving on to the more interpretive and creative work in the Activities Book. They should, of course, be answered without reference to the text.

d) *Using the Activities Book*

There is no special teacher's edition of the book; the text in the numbered paragraphs which give instructions for exploiting the material is addressed principally to the students, with occasional comments for the teacher's benefit. The students are thus directly involved at every stage. Many of the phrases and sentences given as examples for functional use provide a suitable medium for chorus work. Obviously, only a selection of examples is given and even these will prove too many for some students; it should be emphasized at the outset that they are not expected at this stage to retain everything for active use but rather to select those examples which they find easiest to handle.

Some Units include brain-storming sessions: students race a time limit to put forward ideas on a topic. The results can then be used for further role-plays, structure practice and vocabulary development.

In the early Units, the activities concentrate on exercising one function at a time, but as the course proceeds and the activities become more complex a number of functions may overlap. As functions first encountered at an earlier stage recur in later Units, students are reminded of these and encouraged to revise the techniques practised earlier. Teachers should take every opportunity of pointing out as they arise, situations where particular 'functional techniques' are appropriate.

One of the most difficult problems in compiling the Activities Book has been to decide what to leave out. So many possibilities exist for role-playing, communication and comprehension exercises that it would be quite impossible to include or even envisage them all. Individual teachers and groups will, using their combined knowledge and experience, continually discover fresh possibilities for themselves.

Some of the texts and examples in the Activities Book contain language structures which have not yet appeared in the corresponding episodes. To limit the material in this way would have been totally impracticable and self-defeating since—as pointed out in paragraph 2: 'Course Level'—many students will approach the course with quite an advanced passive knowledge. Activities which the teacher judges too difficult in their actual position in the course may be tackled later; articles which can be only superficially understood at a first reading may be studied again in more depth as the students' mastery of the language increases.

A number of the suggestions lend themselves naturally to written work; others, such as the more complex role-playing exercises, will require advance preparation to give the students time to research the background to the project in question. The teacher's help will naturally be needed extensively at first but the ultimate aim should be for the teacher to retreat into the background while the activity is in progress, giving help and guidance when necessary but as far as possible reserving comments and criticism until the end. The articles for reading comprehension may be prepared by the students in advance or dealt with as a group exercise.

At all times the students should be encouraged to extend their knowledge by active effort and involvement in the course, rather than by passive acceptance of the teacher's contribution.

1 The First Day

Introduction

Discovery Engineering Limited is a light engineering company. Its head office and factory are in Birmingham and it has sales offices in London, Glasgow and Bristol. The company is expanding rapidly and from time to time it recruits young graduates and trains them in management skills. They are called *management trainees*. For their first few months with the company they go from one department to another and learn about company policy and organization. Mr Green is one of the directors of Discovery Engineering; he is responsible for Management Services. He looks after the trainees and supervises their training programme.

David Long is 25 years old. He's a management trainee. To-day is his first day. Sheila Smith is 24. She's a management trainee as well. To-day is her first day too. David and Sheila are in Reception. They're talking to each other.

Dialogue

DAVID: How do you do! My name's David Long.
SHEILA: I'm pleased to meet you, David. I'm Sheila Smith.
DAVID: Nice to meet you, Sheila. I'm a new management trainee. This is my first day.
SHEILA: I'm a new management trainee as well. This is my first day too.
DAVID: Let's ask the receptionist to tell Mr Green we're here . . .
SHEILA: Yes, all right.
DAVID: Good morning.
RECEPTIONIST: Good morning.
DAVID: My name's David Long. This is Sheila Smith. We're new management trainees. To-day is our first day. Will you please tell Mr Green we're here?
RECEPTIONIST: Certainly—one moment please . . . (on phone) Good morning Mr Green. This is Reception. Mr Long and Miss Smith are here. They're new management trainees. To-day is their first day . . . Yes, all right, I'll send them up (puts phone down) . . . Will you please go up to Mr Green's office? It's number 28, on the second floor. The lift is over there.
SHEILA: Thank you.
DAVID: Thanks very much.
RECEPTIONIST: That's all right!

Lesson Notes

To recruit = to find (for example, by advertising) and employ
To look after = to attend to the needs of (a person), to be responsible for
To tell (someone something) = to inform
I'll send them up = I'll ask them to come up (to your office).
Will you please ...? is a polite way of asking a person to do something.
What kind of ...? A question beginning with these words calls for a description or identification of something or someone.
management skills = a skill is the ability to perform a certain function or activity effectively and well.

Informal Greetings

David and Sheila are young people of the same age and background and it is natural for them to use each other's first names as soon as they meet. When David first speaks to Sheila he uses the conventional phrase *How do you do?* It is quite usual for both parties to an introduction to say *How do you do?* and to shake hands, and no further greeting is necessary. But many people, and young people in particular, prefer to use the less formal *I'm pleased to meet you, Glad to meet you, Nice to know you* or even just *Hullo* when meeting others of their own age. *How do you do?* is always correct and when you first come to England you should use this form of greeting until you become familiar with English habits. It is not customary in England to shake hands with friends and colleagues whom we meet frequently, either socially or at work.

Grammar

The main points introduced in this Episode are:
1. Simple present tense of verbs (with short forms where used)
2. Present continuous tense
3. Imperative mood
4. Formation of questions
5. Personal pronouns and possessive adjectives

(The numbers refer to the sections in the grammar notes.)

Drills
A
SPEAKER: Good morning. Welcome to this school. You're here to study English. To-day is your first day. Now, I'm speaking to another student. Listen.
Good morning.
ACTOR: Good morning.
SPEAKER: Welcome to this school.

ACTOR: Thank you.
SPEAKER: What's your name?
ACTOR: My name's Thomas Braun.
SPEAKER: Are you studying English?
ACTOR: Yes, I am.
SPEAKER: Is to-day your first day?
ACTOR: Yes, it is.
SPEAKER: Well, good luck with your studies.
ACTOR: Thank you very much.
SPEAKER: Now, I'm speaking to YOU again. Try to answer me in the same way. Give your own name when I ask you.
Good morning.
Welcome to this school.
What's your name?
Are you studying English?
Is to-day your first day?
Well, good luck with your studies.

B

David Long.   My name's David Long.   How do you do?   My name's David Long.

Sheila Smith.   I'm Sheila Smith.   meet you David.   I'm Sheila Smith.   I'm pleased to meet you David.   I'm Sheila Smith.

Sheila.   meet you, Sheila.   Nice to meet you, Sheila.

we're here?   tell Mr Green we're here?   Will you please tell Mr Green we're here?

office?   Mr Green's office?   go up to Mr Green's office?
Will you please go up to Mr Green's office?

over there.   The lift is over there.
Thank you very much.
That's all right!

C

Examples

To-day is David's first day.   This is his first day.
To-day is Sheila's first day.   This is her first day.

To-day is my first day.
To-day is David and Sheila's
first day.
To-day is your first day.

To-day is your and your fellow
students' first day.
Is to-day your first day?

D

Examples

I'm a new management trainee.	I'm a new management trainee too.
I work for Discovery Engineering.	I work for Discovery Engineering too.

I live in Birmingham.
I'm learning English.
I'm learning to drive a car.
I like England.
I like learning English.

Comprehension

1. What kind of company is Discovery Engineering Ltd?
2. Where is its factory?
3. Where is its head office?
4. Where are its sales offices?
5. Who does it recruit from time to time?
6. What are these people called?
7. Who is David Long?
8. Who is Sheila Smith?
9. Who is Mr Green?
10. How old is David?
11. How old is Sheila?
12. What is Mr Green responsible for?

2 In Mr Green's Office

Introduction

The receptionist directs David and Sheila to Mr Green's office. It's a pleasant office on the second floor, at the front of the building. Its window overlooks the car park. Mr Green is about fifty; he has grey hair and he wears glasses. He's wearing a blue suit with a white shirt and a striped tie, and he's smoking a cigarette. Mr Green is going to tell David and Sheila where they are going to work during their first few weeks. When they come into his office he gets up and shakes hands with them.

Dialogue

GREEN: How do you do, Miss Smith? How do you do, Mr Long? My name's Green.
DAVID:
SHEILA: } How do you do, Mr Green?
GREEN: Please sit down. Welcome to Discovery Engineering. I hope you're going to enjoy working for us.
DAVID: Thank you.
SHEILA: Thank you very much.
GREEN: Would you like a cigarette?
SHEILA: Not for me, thank you. I don't smoke.
GREEN: How about you, Mr Long?
DAVID: Yes please.
GREEN: Here's a light.
DAVID: Thanks very much.
GREEN: Now, I expect you're both wondering which departments you're going to work in!
SHEILA:
DAVID: } Yes, we are.
GREEN: Well, Miss Smith, you're going to start in the Marketing Department. Mr Blake is the Sales and Marketing Director. Mr Long, you're going to start in the Advertising Section. Mrs Wood is in charge there. Now, have you any questions?
DAVID: Is there a staff canteen?
GREEN: Yes, there is. It's a very good one. It's on the ground floor. Now, my secretary is going to take you to your new offices. Good luck to you both!
SHEILA:
DAVID: } Thank you, Mr Green.

Lesson Notes

I expect you're both wondering = I think/suppose/am sure that you're both wondering.
We often use *expect* in this way. It can also mean *to wait for something that we are almost sure will happen*—for example: *I'm expecting a letter from my insurance company*. Notice that we say *Mr Green wears glasses* (a permanent feature) but *he's wearing a blue suit* ... (on this particular day).
Mrs Wood is in charge = Mrs Wood is the head of the section.
How about ...? is an idiomatic way of introducing a subject or a person into a conversation, of making a suggestion or asking an opinion. For example: *I like working here. How about you?* = Do you like working here as well? Sometimes we say *What about ...?* instead of *How about ...?* There is no difference in the meaning.
To tell (someone to do something) = to order, instruct, command. Compare with the use of *to tell* in Episode 1.

Grammar

The main points introduced in this Episode are:
6   *going to* + infinitive
7   Prepositions *in* and *into*
8   Formation of negatives
9   Possessive forms
10 Object forms (direct and indirect) of personal pronouns
11 The impersonal pronoun *one* (pl. *ones*)

Drills

A

down.	sit down.	Please sit down.
cigarette?	like a cigarette?	Would you like a cigarette?
thank you.	for me, thank you.	Not for me, thank you.
Mr Long?	you, Mr Long?	How about you, Mr Long?
questions?	any questions?	Have you any questions?
canteen?	staff canteen?	Is there a staff canteen?

B

Examples

Is Mr Green a Director?	Yes, he is.
Are David and Sheila trainees?	Yes, they are.

6

Are you learning English?
Is Sheila a management trainee?
Are you and your fellow students learning English?
Is Mr Green's office on the second floor?
Am I a teacher?

C

Examples

Ask me where the head office is.	Where's the head office?
Ask me where David works.	Where does David work?

Ask me where I work.
Ask me where the factory is.
Ask me where David and Sheila work.
Ask me where the sales offices are.

D

Examples

Tell me to speak slowly.	Speak slowly!
Ask me politely to speak slowly.	Will you please speak slowly?

Tell me to listen to you.
Ask me politely to listen to you.
Tell me to close the window.
Ask me politely to close the window.
Tell me to open the door.
Ask me politely to open the door.

E

Examples

Is David a director?	No, he isn't.
Does Mr Green smoke a pipe?	No, he doesn't.

Is Mr Green's office on the ground floor?
Are Sheila and David directors?

Do Sheila and David work in
London?
Is Sheila a receptionist?
Are you a teacher?
Am I a student?
Are we speaking Chinese?
Do you live in England?

Comprehension

1. Where is Mr Green's office?
2. Is it at the back of the building?
3. Does the window overlook the road?
4. About how old is Mr Green?
5. What is he wearing?
6. What does he do when David and Sheila come in?
7. What is he going to tell them?
8. Does Mr Green smoke?
9. Does he smoke a pipe?
10. Does Sheila smoke?
11. Where is David going to work?
12. Where is Sheila going to work?
13. Is Mr Green's office on the third floor?
14. Is Mr Green wearing a brown suit?

3 First Assignments

Introduction

Mr Green's secretary's name is Ruth. She's a dark-haired girl with brown eyes and she's dressed in a blue tweed skirt and a white blouse. Ruth is taking David and Sheila to their new jobs in the Advertising Section and the Marketing Department. Both of these are on the fourth floor, and they go up in the lift. When they come out of the lift they see two glass doors. The one on the right is marked *Advertising* and the one on the left is marked *Marketing*.

David and Sheila wish each other good luck. Ruth takes Sheila into the Marketing Department while David waits on the landing. When Ruth comes back, she and David go through the door marked *Advertising*. Ruth introduces David to the Section Head, Mrs Wood. She's a smart, attractive woman in her forties, with brown hair and hazel eyes. She's busy rearranging the furniture in her office, and David offers to help her.

Dialogue

RUTH: Good morning, Mrs Wood. This is Mr Long, one of the new management trainees. Mr Long—Mrs Wood.
DAVID: I'm pleased to meet you, Mrs Wood.
MRS WOOD: Pleased to meet you, Mr Long. Thank you, Ruth.
RUTH: Not at all. Good-bye for now, Mr Long.
DAVID: Good-bye. Thanks for your help.
RUTH: Don't mention it.
MRS WOOD: Excuse the muddle! I'm just changing the layout of my office. I want to have my desk and chair near the window.
DAVID: Can I help you? I'm here to make myself useful.
MRS WOOD: That's very kind of you. Now, I'll have the filing cabinet behind the desk and the table against the opposite wall.
DAVID: Shall I put these filing trays on your desk?
MRS WOOD: I think I'll arrange those myself. The waste paper basket can go under the table. I'll have this lamp on the table and those chairs can stand in that corner.
DAVID: Is that all right?
MRS WOOD: That's fine! Now, let's have a cup of coffee. There's a machine on the landing, opposite the lift.
DAVID: Are there any cups?

MRS WOOD: Yes, there are some disposable ones on a shelf beside the machine.
DAVID: Good. You sit down and I'll fetch two cups of coffee right away.

Lesson Notes

a dark-haired girl = a girl with dark hair. A number of nouns may take the suffix *-ed* to form adjectives. For example: a bearded man, a long-tailed cat
To be dressed in = to be wearing
Mrs Wood is busy rearranging her office. To be busy + the *-ing* form of a verb denoting an activity means *to be occupied in that activity: to be doing the action suggested by the verb.*
Disposable cups = cups which are thrown away (disposed of) after use
What does ... look like? This type of question calls for a description of the appearance of someone or something.
Those chairs can stand in the corner = the corner is a convenient place for the chairs to be placed. Anything which is taller than its base, and is stable, can be said to stand. The verb can also be used transitively, and means *to put or place upright.*
You sit down and I'll fetch two cups of coffee ... This idiomatic construction begins with an imperative: (*You*) *sit down* ...
However, it is *not* a command, but a friendly suggestion which is followed by the action which the *speaker* intends to perform. In this context, it shows a helpful and considerate attitude on the part of the speaker (David) towards his superior (Mrs Wood) and the same words could be spoken to a colleague. Sometimes, however, this construction is used to suggest how work or other activities may be shared between two or more people, and would only be appropriate when speaking to colleagues or subordinates. Some further examples are given in Drill D.

Grammar

The main points introduced in this Episode are:
12   Emphatic and reflexive pronouns
13   Demonstratives *this, that, these* and *those*
14   Adjectives—order and position
15   *Can*
16   Future tense
17   *Will* used to imply habit, tendency, refusal to do or stop doing something. This use is not actually demonstrated in the Episode, but it is explained in the grammar notes with other uses of *will*.

18   Questions introduced by *how*
19   Questions introduced by *what, where, who* and *how* when followed by a verb needing *do* as auxiliary for the formation of questions.

Drills

A

Mrs Wood.   Good morning, Mrs Wood.

Mr Long.   This is Mr Long.   Mr Long—Mrs Wood.

Mrs Wood.   to meet you, Mrs Wood.
I'm pleased to meet you, Mrs Wood.

your help.   Thanks for your help.

Don't mention it.

kind of you.   very kind of you.   That's very kind of you.

on your desk?   these filing trays on your desk?
Shall I put these filing trays on your desk?

cup of coffee.   have a cup of coffee.
Now let's have a cup of coffee.

right away.   two cups of coffee right away.   I'll fetch two cups of coffee right away.
You sit down and I'll fetch two cups of coffee right away.

B

Examples

I'll have the desk near the window.	Put the desk near the window, please.
I'll have the chair behind the desk.	Put the chair behind the desk, please.

I'll have the telephone on the desk.
I'll have these chairs in the corner.
I'll have those filing trays on the table.
I'll have this lamp on the table.
I'll have the waste paper basket under the desk.

C

Examples
The desk can go near the window.	Will you please put the desk near the window?
The chair can go behind the desk.	Will you please put the chair behind the desk?

The telephone can go on the desk.
Those chairs can go in the corner.
These filing trays can go on the table.
This table can go against the wall.
That lamp can go on the table.

D

Examples
Wait here. I'll answer the phone.	You wait here and I'll answer the phone.
Sit down. I'll fetch some coffee.	You sit down and I'll fetch some coffee.

Answer those letters. I'll do the filing.
Put the books away. I'll tidy the desk.
Type the letters. I'll go to the bank.

Comprehension

1. What is Mr Green's secretary's name?
2. What does she look like?
3. Where is the Marketing Department?
4. Where is the Advertising Section?
5. How do Ruth, Sheila and David reach the fourth floor?
6. What do they see when they come out of the lift?
7. Where does Ruth take Sheila?
8. Where does David wait?
9. How is Ruth dressed?
10. Who does Ruth introduce David to?
11. What does Mrs Wood look like?
12. About how old is she?
13. What is she doing when Ruth and David arrive?
14. What does David offer to do?

4 David Asks Some Questions

Introduction

David goes to the vending machine on the landing and gets two cups of coffee, one for Mrs Wood and one for himself. Mrs Wood takes her coffee black, without sugar; David likes his coffee white, with sugar. While they are drinking their coffee, David asks Mrs Wood a lot of questions about Discovery Engineering and especially about its Advertising Section. Mrs Wood explains to him how the section is organized and how it functions, and she also tells him something about the Company's policy on advertising in general. David learns a number of new expressions which have a particular meaning in the world of advertising.

Dialogue

MRS WOOD: Well now, Mr Long—do you know anything about advertising?
DAVID: Nothing at all, really. Of course, I see a lot of commercials on TV and adverts in the press and so on, but I don't suppose that's quite what you mean.
MRS WOOD: No, not really. Almost all our customers are industrial users, so we rarely advertise in the mass media.
DAVID: I suppose you advertise in the trade journals?
MRS WOOD: That's right. Our products are used by a very wide range of industries. We advertise in most of the principal trade journals, and in some of the professional ones too.
DAVID: Do you handle all the advertising yourselves, or do you use an agency?
MRS WOOD: We handle it ourselves. We also produce our own sales literature.
DAVID: Do you employ any artists?
MRS WOOD: We have one. She's known as a 'visualizer'. We also have a copywriter; he takes any photographs we need as well. We're all kept pretty busy.
DAVID: Surely you don't do your own printing?
MRS WOOD: Good gracious no! For prestige brochures and anything with a lot of art-work or colour, we use Printall Ltd. in the city centre. Simple, run-of-the-mill things like price lists and instruction sheets are done by a small, local firm.
DAVID: How are photographs and drawings reproduced?
MRS WOOD: Special blocks have to be made. They're very expensive. Look, here's a set of our current literature. Why

13

don't you sit down at that table and browse through it? You'll learn a lot about the Company and its products.

Lesson Notes

to get has a number of meanings and is also used in many phrases (sometimes referred to as *phrasal verbs*). Some examples of such phrases occur in Episode 5.
Here, *to get* = to fetch, buy, obtain.
I don't suppose that's quite what you mean = I think you probably mean something quite different.
Sales literature = catalogues, brochures etc. which describe a company's products or services.
pretty busy = moderately or fairly busy. This use of *pretty* as an adverb qualifying an adjective is common in spoken English. Compare: a pretty old cottage = an old cottage which is also pretty with: That cottage is pretty old.
She's known as a 'visualizer'. A *visual* in commercial art is a rough drawing or painting which gives an idea or impression of the finished work. In an advertising department, much of the artist's work consists of preparing such *visuals*, and he or she is sometimes given the job title of *visualizer*.
Surely you don't do your own printing! The speaker is almost sure that the response to this remark will be *no*.
own is an adjective emphasizing possession. Compare: This is my house (= the house where I live) and: This is my own house (= I am the owner of this house.
In this episode, *own* is used to emphasize the fact that the company does not actually print its advertising material, but only prepares the copy.
run-of-the-mill = ordinary
Why don't you ...? is an idiomatic way of making a suggestion. Here are some further examples:
Why don't you take an aspirin for your headache? (= I suggest you take ...)
Why don't we go to the cinema? (= Would you like to go ...?)
to browse through (books, papers, photographs etc.) = to study quietly, without haste

Grammar
The main points introduced in this Episode are:
20   Questions beginning with *why*
21   *How, what, where* and *who* as conjunctions
22   *some* and *any*
23   *something* and *anything*
24   Relative pronoun *what*

25 Formation of adverbs
26 *Have to* and *have got to*/+ infinitive
27 The passive voice

Drills

A

advertising?   about advertising?   anything about advertising?
Do you know anything about advertising?

what you mean.   quite what you mean.   that's quite what you mean.
I don't suppose that's quite what you mean.

trade journals?   in the trade journals?   advertise in the trade journals?
I suppose you advertise in the trade journals?

yourselves?   advertising yourselves?   all the advertising yourselves?
Do you handle all the advertising yourselves?

artists?   employ any artists?   Do you employ any artists?

printing?   your own printing?   don't do your own printing?
Surely you don't do your own printing?

through it?   browse through it?   at that table and browse through it?   sit down at that table and browse through it?
Why don't you sit down at that table and browse through it?

B

Examples
Ask me how the section is organized.
Ask me how I take my coffee.

How is the section organized?
How do you take your coffee?

Ask me how much I know about advertising.
Ask me how Mrs Wood takes her coffee.
Ask me how the office is arranged.
Ask me how David takes his coffee.
Ask me how old David is.

15

Ask me where the vending machine is.
Ask me if there are any cups.
Ask me if there's a canteen.

C

Examples

This is how we organize the section.
This is how we arrange the office.

This is how the section is organized.
This is how the office is arranged.

This is how we make the blocks.
This is where we do the work.
This is where we keep the books.
This is where we buy our stationery.
This is where we print the leaflets.
This is how we write the copy.

D

Examples

Please tell me how you organize the section.
Please tell David how we make the blocks.

Please tell me how the section is organized.
Please tell David how the blocks are made.

Please tell David how we arrange the office.
Please tell the trainees how to write the copy.
Please tell my new secretary where you keep the stationery.
Please tell Sheila where we file the brochures.

Comprehension

1 Where is the coffee vending machine?
2 How does Mrs Wood like her coffee?
3 How does David take his coffee?
4 Does David know anything about advertising?

5   Where does he see commercials?
6   Where does he see other advertisements?
7   Where does Discovery Engineering advertise its products?
8   Who uses the products of Discovery Engineering?
9   Does Discovery Engineering produce its own sales literature?
10 Does it use an advertising agency?
11 Does it do its own printing?
12 Where are its brochures and price lists printed?

5 David Gets Down To Work

Introduction

David arrives at the office punctually at nine o'clock the following morning and goes straight up to the Advertising Section. In the lift he meets Sheila and he asks her how she is getting on. She says that she is getting on all right and he suggests that they have lunch together and compare notes. Sheila agrees and they arrange to meet at one o'clock outside the canteen. When the lift reaches the fourth floor they go to their respective offices.

Mrs Wood is already in her office and she is looking worried. Some proofs are overdue and she tells David to telephone the printers to find out the reason for the delay.

Dialogue

DAVID: Good morning, Mrs Wood. Is there something the matter? You're looking very worried.

MRS WOOD: Good morning, David. Yes, there is. The proofs for the new sales brochure are supposed to be here to-day, but they aren't in this morning's post. The brochure's needed in two weeks' time. It's getting urgent.

DAVID: Perhaps they're still in the post room. Shall I go and find out?

MRS WOOD: Yes please. If they're not there, will you get on to the printers right away? The number's in the book by the phone ... (*pause—sound of door opening and closing*)

DAVID: They aren't in the post room. I'll ring the printers. Let's see now ... Printall ... here we are: 2468 1357 ... (*dials*)

PRINTALL EMPLOYEE: Good morning. Printall Ltd. Can I help you?

DAVID: Good morning. Discovery Engineering here. My name's Long, Advertising Section. We're expecting some proofs from you. They're supposed to be here to-day but they're not in this morning's post.

PRINTALL EMPLOYEE: Hold the line please—I'll put you through to the office ...

CLERK: General office.

DAVID: Good morning. My name's Long, of the Advertising Section of Discovery Engineering. I'm enquiring about some proofs we're expecting from you. They're supposed to be here this morning but they're not in the post.

CLERK: Just a moment please ... Hullo!

DAVID: Yes?
CLERK: Your proofs are being delivered by our own van this morning. You'll have them by half-past ten.
DAVID: Oh, fine! Thank you very much. Good-bye. *(hangs up)* The proofs will be here by half-past ten, Mrs Wood.
MRS WOOD: Thank goodness for that! Now let's get down to some work!

Lesson Notes

David goes straight up to the office = goes there directly, without delay

The general enquiry *How are you getting on?* is usually taken to mean: *Are you happy?* or *Are you enjoying your work?* and commonly receives such replies as *Oh fine, thank you* or *Not too badly, thanks*. A specific question beginning with *How are you getting on with ...?* and related to a particular activity or piece of work, calls for a report on one's progress with the project.

To get on well with someone = to be on good terms with, have a good relationship with that person

To compare notes = to exchange news, ideas, information etc.

To look worried (tired, angry etc.) = to have the appearance of being worried etc.

The proofs are supposed to be here = the proofs are expected, promised or awaited.

To get urgent = to become urgent. Similarly: to get tired = to become tired

To get better = to become well again after an illness, to improve

To find out = to obtain information, to learn a fact or the reason for something

Will you get on to the printers right away? = Will you telephone the printers immediately?

To get down to work = to begin work, to give serious attention to one's work

Yes, he does look ill. The auxiliary *do* is used here for emphasis. Further examples of the emphatic use of *do* occur in future Episodes and are explained in detail in Grammar Note 45.

Drills

A

the matter? something the matter? Is there something the matter?
worried! looking very worried! You're looking very worried! Is there something the matter? You're looking very worried!

post room.   in the post room.   still in the post room.
Perhaps they're still in the post room.
find out?   go and find out?   Shall I go and find out?
Perhaps they're still in the post room.   Shall I go and find out?

right away?   the printers right away?   get on to the printers right away?   will you get on to the printers right away?
If they're not there, will you get on to the printers right away?

the office.   through to the office.   I'll put you through to the office.
Hold the line, please;   I'll put you through to the office.

this morning.   our own van this morning.   being delivered by our own van this morning.
Your proofs are being delivered by our own van this morning.

half-past ten.   here by half-past ten.   The proofs will be here by half-past ten.

B

Examples
Sheila is happy in the Marketing Department.
David likes working in the Advertising Section.

Sheila is getting on well in the Marketing Department.
David is getting on well in the Advertising Section.

The copywriter is making good progress with the advertisement.
Sheila likes working for Mr Blake.
David likes working for Mrs Wood.
Sheila is making progress with her work.
Sheila doesn't like the copywriter.
David doesn't like the secretary.
Mrs Wood is starting her work.

C

Examples
I think Mrs Wood is worried.
I think the secretary is ill.

Yes, she looks worried.
Yes, she looks ill.

I think David is happy.
I think Sheila and her friends are tired.
I think Mr Blake is angry.
I think this office is untidy.

D

Examples

Mrs Wood is looking worried.　　Yes, she does look worried.
The secretary is looking ill.　　Yes, she does look ill.

David is looking unhappy.
Sheila and her friends are
looking tired.
Mr Blake is looking angry.
The secretaries are looking smart.

E

Examples

I think David is unhappy.　　What's the matter with him?
I think Mrs Wood is worried.　　What's the matter with her?

I think Mr Blake is upset.
I hear the secretaries are
complaining.
This machine is out of order.
These proofs are no good.

Comprehension

1　What time does David arrive at the office?
2　Does he arrive late?
3　Where does he meet Sheila?
4　What do Sheila and David arrange to do?
5　Do they arrange to meet inside the canteen?
6　How does Mrs Wood look when David arrives?
7　Why is she worried?
8　What does she tell David to do?
9　What does he do first?
10　What does the clerk at Printall tell David?
11　What time will the proofs arrive?
12　What does Mrs Wood say when David tells her the news?

6 Lunch In The Canteen

Introduction

Punctually at one o'clock David goes down to the ground floor and arrives at the entrance to the canteen. A few moments later Sheila appears and they go into the canteen together. While they are eating their meal they compare notes on the things they have learned so far. David discovers that the Advertising Section is part of the Marketing Department. In fact, Mrs Wood is responsible to Mr Blake, the Sales and Marketing Director.

After lunch they go for a stroll. The factory is built on a modern industrial estate on the outskirts of the city, and there are pleasant views of the countryside all around.

Dialogue

DAVID: Ah, there you are!
SHEILA: I hope I haven't kept you waiting.
DAVID: Not at all! I've only just got here myself. Let's see what's on the menu to-day.
SHEILA: I think I'll have the roast lamb with peas and roast potatoes.
CANTEEN WORKER: Would you like some mint sauce with the lamb?
SHEILA: Just a little, please ... thank you.
DAVID: What's the steak and kidney pie like?
CANTEEN WORKER: It's very good to-day.
DAVID: Then I'll try it.
CANTEEN WORKER: Mashed potatoes or chips?
DAVID: Chips, please. Have you any beans?
CANTEEN WORKER: I'm sorry, we haven't any beans to-day. How about some peas?
DAVID: All right, I'll have a few peas, please.
CANTEEN WORKER: What about a sweet?
SHEILA: No sweet for me, thank you. Just coffee.
DAVID: Two coffees, please .. Let's sit here, shall we? Well, how do you like working for Discovery Engineering?
SHEILA: Very much indeed. Everyone's so friendly. How about you?
DAVID: Oh, I'm getting on fine. I've spent most of this morning chasing proofs and studying the sales literature.
SHEILA: I've been looking through the sales literature as well. It seems that your section is part of the Marketing

Department. In fact, Mr Blake is Mrs Wood's boss. He's the Sales and Marketing Director, you know.
DAVID: Of course he is—I remember Mr Green telling us; advertising is just part of the whole business of marketing, isn't it?
SHEILA: That's right.
DAVID: Do you know that they're introducing a new product very soon?
SHEILA: Mr Blake says that they're introducing new products all the time.
DAVID: The company certainly makes a very wide range of products. No wonder they need their own advertising section! Have you finished your lunch?
SHEILA: Yes thanks. This is quite a good canteen, isn't it?
DAVID: Not bad at all. What about a stroll before we start work again?
SHEILA: Good idea! It's a lovely day!

Lesson Notes

To discover = to learn, to become aware of for the first time
Mrs Wood is responsible to Mr Blake = Mr Blake is Mrs Wood's immediate superior. Compare with *to be responsible for* = to be in charge of
to go for a stroll = to take a short, unhurried walk for pleasure or relaxation
To keep someone waiting = to cause them to wait by arriving late for an appointment
To get to a place = to arrive at that place
just coffee = only coffee
I've been chasing proofs = I've been trying to locate them, to find out when they will arrive, etc.
to look through = to read, examine (but not very closely)

Grammar

The main points introduced in this Episode are:
28 Prepositions *to* and *at*
29 Formation of past participle of regular verbs
30 Formation of present perfect tense
31 Use of present perfect tense
32 Formation of present perfect continuous tense
33 Use of present perfect continuous tense
34 Present participle/verbal noun (the *ing* form)
35 *a little, a few, much, many, a lot of*

Drills

A

there you are!   Ah, there you are!
waiting.   kept you waiting.   haven't kept you waiting.
Ah, there you are!   I hope I haven't kept you waiting.

myself.   got here myself.   just got here myself.   I've only just got here myself.
Not at all!   I've only just got here myself.

Discovery Engineering?   working for Discovery Engineering?   like working for Discovery Engineering?
How do you like working for Discovery Engineering?

isn't it?   business of marketing, isn't it?   just part of the whole business of marketing, isn't it?
Advertising is just part of the whole business of marketing, isn't it?

section.   advertising section.   they need their own advertising section.   No wonder they need their own advertising section!

isn't it?   good canteen, isn't it?   This is quite a good canteen, isn't it?

again?   start work again?   stroll before we start work again?
What about a stroll before we start work again?

B

Examples

How has David spent the morning? (read)   He's been reading.

How has Sheila spent the morning? (telephone)   She's been telephoning.

How have Mr Blake and Mr Green spent the morning? (work)
How has Ruth spent the morning? (type)
How have you spent the morning? (learn English)
How have you and your friends spent the morning? (study)
How have I spent the morning? (teach)

C

Examples

Have you any beans?	Yes, we've got some beans.
Have you any chips?	Yes, we've got some chips.

Have you any mint sauce?
Have you any sugar?
Have you any coffee?
Have you any roast potatoes?

D

Examples

Ask for some beans.	Are there any beans?
Ask for some mint sauce.	Is there any mint sauce?

Ask for some chips.
Ask for some sugar.
Ask for some roast potatoes.
Ask for some coffee.

E

Examples

What about some beans?	Just a few, please.
What about some mint sauce?	Just a little, please.

What about some chips?
What about some sugar?
What about some coffee?
What about some roast potatoes?

F

Examples

I'd like some beans, please.	I'm sorry, there aren't any.
I'd like some mint sauce, please.	I'm sorry, there isn't any.

I'd like some chips, please.
I'd like some sugar, please.
I'd like some coffee, please.
I'd like some roast potatoes, please.

Comprehension

1. What time do David and Sheila meet?
2. Who arrives first?
3. Has Sheila kept David waiting?
4. What's on the menu to-day?
5. How much mint sauce does Sheila want with her roast lamb?
6. What do Sheila and David talk about over lunch?
7. How do they like working for Discovery Engineering?
8. What is Sheila's impression of her new colleagues?
9. How have Sheila and David spent the morning?
10. Who is Mrs Wood responsible to?
11. What is Mrs Wood responsible for?
12. Why isn't David surprised that Discovery Engineering needs its own advertising department?
13. Which department does the Advertising section belong to?
14. What is the relationship between advertising and marketing?
15. What do Sheila and David think of the canteen?
16. What do they do after lunch?
17. In what kind of area are Discovery Engineering's premises?

7 Advertising a New Product

Introduction

Next day, Mrs Wood shows David the drawings and technical data of a new product that will be introduced shortly. She asks him to try his hand at preparing a draft for an advertising leaflet. She impresses on him that the product is still on the secret list, and that he must not discuss it outside the office. If he has any questions about it, he can ask Mr Blake. David is pleased with this suggestion as it will give him an opportunity to go and see Sheila.

Dialogue

DAVID: Hullo, Sheila! I've got my first real job. I have to draft a leaflet for Product BI99. Can you give me some background information on it?

SHEILA: I can't help you myself, but I'm sure Mr Blake can. Ah, here he is! Mr Blake, this is David Long, my fellow trainee. He's working in Mrs Wood's section. He's after some background information on Product BI99.

BLAKE: Pleased to meet you, Mr Long. Come into my office. Now, what do you want to know?

DAVID: Well, I have the diagrams and the technical data, but I'd like a general description of the product. What kind of image do you want to convey? What special features should I emphasize?

BLAKE: The main attraction of this product is economy. Several new design features make it more efficient than many similar, more expensive products made by our competitors.

DAVID: Shall I include some performance data?

BLAKE: Some performance data—yes, that's a very good idea. Here are the results of the tests on the prototype. There isn't a production model available yet.

DAVID: What about prices?

BLAKE: We haven't finalized them yet. Anyway, they'll be on a separate sheet. You needn't worry about them for the time being.

DAVID: I think that's all I need for the moment, thank you.

BLAKE: Has Mrs Wood said anything about photographs?

DAVID: No, she hasn't. Do you want me to include some?

BLAKE: Yes, I think so. A photograph gives a better impression than just a diagram. Have a word with her about it, will you?

DAVID: Yes, of course.

Lesson Notes

to try one's hand at something = to do it for the first time
to impress (something on someone) = to emphasize, when speaking to a person, the importance or significance of a matter
He's after some background information = he wants, is looking for, some information about the origin or history of something.
What kind of image do you want to convey? = What impression do you want people to receive when they read about the product?
A production model = a sample of a product taken from a normal production run
for the time being = for the present, until some time in the future.
Have a word with her about it, will you? = Will you speak to her/ask her about it?

Grammar

The main points dealt with in this Episode are:
36 *Must* and *must not* (*mustn't*)
37 *Need* and *need not* (*needn't*)
38 Comparison of adjectives (and adverbs)
39 Passive voice—future tense
40 *should* expressing obligation

Drills

A

real job. first real job. I've got my first real job.
Hullo, Sheila! I've got my first real job.

convey? want to convey? image do you want to convey?
What kind of image do you want to convey?

emphasize? should I emphasize? features should I emphasize?
What special features should I emphasize?

data? performance data? include some performance data?
Shall I include some performance data?

thank you. for the moment, thank you. all I need for the moment, thank you.
I think that's all I need for the moment, thank you.

photographs? anything about photographs?
Has Mrs Wood said anything about photographs?

will you? about it, will you? with her about it, will you?
Have a word with her about it, will you?

B

Examples

Shall we go for a stroll?

Shall I fetch some coffee?

A stroll—yes, that's a very good idea!
Some coffee—yes, that's a very good idea!

Shall I ring the printers?
Shall I include some photographs?
Shall I include some performance data?
Shall we have lunch in the canteen?

C

Examples

What about the new product?

What about prices?

You needn't bother about that for the time being.
You needn't bother about them for the time being.

What about photographs?
What about the new brochure?
What about the prototype?
What about diagrams?

D

Examples

Have you enough photographs?

Have you enough information?

These are all the photographs I need for the moment, thank you.
This is all the information I need for the moment, thank you.

Have you enough brochures?
Have you enough stationery?
Have you enough diagrams?
Have you enough sales literature?

E

Examples

What about a general description of the product?	Yes, I'd like a general description of the product, please.
What about some technical data?	Yes, I'd like some technical data, please.

What about some performance data?
What about a prototype?
What about some photographs?
What about a diagram?

Comprehension

1. What is David's 'first real job' at Discovery Engineering?
2. Why is it confidential?
3. Where can David obtain further information on BI99?
4. Why does he welcome the chance to visit Mr Blake's department?
5. Can Sheila give him the information he wants?
6. Who does she refer him to?
7. What information does he want?
8. How does Mr Blake describe BI99?
9. What test results does he give to David?
10. Why can't he give David details of the prices?
11. Does Mr Blake want photographs included in the new leaflet? Why?
12. How will David obtain the photographs he needs?

8 Selling and Marketing

Introduction

When David comes out of Mr Blake's room he finds Sheila at a desk in the general office. She has a large pile of new sales literature to sort out and put into folders for the sales representatives. On the wall behind her is a map of the British Isles, showing the regions covered by the four sales offices. The representatives who work from these offices are assigned to various territories within their regions. Each representative has a company car and carries with him a complete range of advertising literature. When a sales office runs short of literature it orders fresh supplies from Head Office. When stocks at Head Office begin to run low, consideration is given to possible amendments before re-ordering.

Dialogue

DAVID: Hullo, what have you got there?
SHEILA: Some of the literature has been up-dated and every salesman has got to have a complete new set.
DAVID: What sort of amendments have been made?
SHEILA: In most cases, the photographs have been changed. It's important for the company's image that everything is modern and in keeping with to-day's trends.
DAVID: That sounds like a bit of sales jargon to me!
SHEILA: Perhaps it is. But you must understand that a company with a name like *Discovery* must have an absolutely modern image.
DAVID: What do you mean by a *modern image*?
SHEILA: Well, it's basically the impression that people have of the company as a whole. Everyone regards Discovery as a very modern, go-ahead company, and everything in connection with our sales presentation should reflect this impression.
DAVID: What other changes are made?
SHEILA: Occasionally a brochure will be printed in a different type-face; now and again a product description will be modified. New applications of the product may be illustrated. Sometimes patent or registered design numbers have to be added.
DAVID: Are all the products patented?

SHEILA: I believe quite a few of them are, but I don't know much about that side of things. That's the Company Secretary's responsibility.
DAVID: I suppose we shall understand it all some day!
SHEILA: Let's hope so!

Lesson Notes

to sort out = to classify, arrange in order
to run short of something = to have only a small quantity left
Compare: to run out of something = to have none left
to run low (subject: a substance or commodity) = to be scarce, less plentiful than formerly
What sort of ...? = What kind of ...? See note to Episode 1.
That sounds like a bit of sales jargon! = In my opinion, you are repeating sales jargon
David is commenting on something he has just heard. We use *to sound like* to refer to something we hear and *to look like* to refer to something we see. Compare: *That sounds like thunder* = I hear a noise which I think is thunder with: *It looks like rain* = From the appearance of the sky I think it is going to rain.
absolutely = completely
Everyone regards Discovery as ... = In everyone's opinion, Discovery is ...
Are all the products patented? I believe quite a few of them are.
This is an extension of the *short answer*; a simple reply to this question is *Yes, they are* but the speaker is giving a qualified reply.

Grammar

The main points introduced in this Episode are:
41   Passive voice—present perfect tense
42   *so* replacing a phrase or sentence

Drills

A

there?   got there?   have you got there?   Hullo, what have you got there?

made?   been made?   amendments have been made?
What sort of amendments have been made?

to-day's trends.   in keeping with to-day's trends.   modern and in keeping with to-day's trends.

image.   company's image.   important for the company's image.

It's important for the company's image that everything is modern and in keeping with to-day's trends.

modern image.   absolute modern image.   must have an absolutely modern image.   Discovery Engineering   name like Discovery Engineering   A company with a name like Discovery Engineering
A company with a name like Discovery Engineering must have an absolutely modern image.

this impression.   should reflect this impression.   our sales presentation should reflect this impression.
Everything in connection with our sales presentation should reflect this impression.

side of things.   much about that side of things.   I don't know much about that side of things.
few of them are,   quite a few of them are,   I believe quite a few of them are,
I believe quite a few of them are, but I don't know much about that side of things.

one day!   understand it all one day!   we shall understand it all one day!
I suppose we shall understand it all one day!

B

Examples

Are all the products patented? (think)	I think so.
Is Discovery an engineering company? (believe)	I believe so.

Will it be fine to-morrow? (hope)
Have the proofs arrived? (hope)
Is Sheila a graduate? (believe)
Does David speak French? (think)
Will the brochure be in colour? (expect)

C

Examples

Are all the products patented?	I believe they are.
Does David work for Mrs Wood?	I believe he does.

Is Mr Blake a director?
Do Sheila and David have lunch in the canteen?
Are Sheila and David graduates?
Is Sheila in Mr Blake's office?

D

Examples

We must have a modern image.	What do you mean by *modern image*?
I'd like some background information.	What do you mean by *background information*?

We need some technical data.
I'm after some performance data.
This literature must be up-dated.
Discovery Engineering is very go-ahead.
This brochure will be printed in a different type-face.
That sounds like a bit of sales jargon!

E

Examples

We're making some changes in the leaflets.	What kind of changes are you making?
We're designing some new products.	What kind of new products are you designing?

We're ordering some new typewriters.
We're looking for some new ideas.
I'm after some background information.
I'm buying a new car.

Comprehension

1. What is Sheila doing with the new sales literature?
2. What does the map behind her desk show?
3. How is the sales team organized?
4. How do the sales offices obtain supplies of literature?
5. What happens before literature is re-ordered?
6. Why is it sometimes necessary to amend sales literature?
7. What kind of amendments are sometimes made?
8. How can sales literature affect a company's image?
9. What kind of image has Discovery Engineering?
10. What can Sheila tell David about patents on the company's products?

9 The Personnel Manager

Introduction

Towards the end of their first week, all management trainees have to go and see the Personnel Manager, Mr Mather. In a brief talk about the company he tells them of the various welfare services offered to the employees; for example, the Pension and Life Assurance Schemes, the Sports and Social Club, the voluntary savings scheme and the payment of wages during sickness.

Sheila and David go along together to Mr Mather's office. After a short, informal talk he gives each of them a booklet containing information on the company and asks them if they have any questions.

Dialogue

MATHER: Ah, Miss Smith, Mr Long! Do come in and sit down.
DAVID:
SHEILA: } Thank you.
MATHER: Now, you've been with us for just one week, I believe. How are you both getting on?
SHEILA: Very well, thank you.
DAVID: Fine, thank you.
MATHER: That's good. Miss Smith, you've been working for Mr Blake, I believe.
SHEILA: Yes, that's right.
MATHER: And you, Mr Long, have been helping Mrs Wood in Advertising.
DAVID: Well, I hope I've been helping!
MATHER: I'm sure you have. But of course, at first you have everything to learn.
DAVID: I certainly have! There's so much to remember, so many new faces, and everything is so new and strange. It's almost like learning a new language.
MATHER: I suppose it is. Now, I'll just tell you briefly about some of the company's services to the staff and then you can ask me some questions if you like. First of all, the pension and life assurance schemes. The latter is free but the former is contributory. You are eligible to join after one year's service. If you are away sick, the company pays full wages for up to one year—less your sickness benefit. You need a doctor's certificate if you are away for more than three days. We also run a voluntary savings scheme and a sports and social club. All these things are fully described in this booklet. Here's a copy each.

35

SHEILA:
DAVID: Thank you.
MATHER: Are there any questions?
DAVID: How do we go about joining the Sports and Social Club?
MATHER: There's a form at the back of the booklet. You fill that in and send it to Miss Morgan, the honorary secretary.
SHEILA: What about the savings scheme?
MATHER: That has to be arranged with the Wages Section. You'll get a form with your first pay cheque. If you want to join, you fill in the form and send it to the Wages Supervisor. Now, is there anything else you'd like to know?
DAVID: What shall we be doing next week?
MATHER: Ah, that's Mr Green's department. I believe he's coming to have a chat with you both this afternoon.

Lesson Notes

It's almost like learning a new language = it is in many respects like, it has certain things in common with, learning a new language.
It's like + the *-ing* form of a verb is often used to compare activities. It can also be used in a negative sense to emphasize the contrast between activities. For example: *Steering a boat isn't like driving a car. Learning to ride a horse isn't like riding a bicycle.*
to be away sick = to be absent from work because of illness
How do we go about joining ...? = What must we do in order to join ...?
You'll get a form = You'll receive a form. *To get* is widely used in this way. For example: *What did you get for your birthday?* = What gifts did you receive?

Grammar

The main points dealt with in this Episode are:
43 *the former* and *the latter*
44 The future continuous tense
45 The emphatic *do*

Drills

A

sit down! come in and sit down! Do come in and sit down! Ah, Mr Long! Do come in and sit down!

I believe. just one week, I believe. with us for just one week, I believe.

Now, you've been with us for just one week, I believe.

I believe.   for Mr Blake, I believe.   working for Mr Blake, I believe.
Miss Smith, you've been working for Mr Blake, I believe.

getting on?   How are you getting on?

social club?   sports and social club?   joining the sports and social club?
go about joining the sports and social club?
How do we go about joining the sports and social club?

Like to know?   anything else you'd like to know?
Is there anything else you'd like to know?

department.   Mr Green's department.   Ah! That's Mr Green's department.
this afternoon.   with you both this afternoon.   have a chat with you both this afternoon.
He's coming to have a chat with you both this afternoon.
Ah! That's Mr Green's department.   He's coming to have a chat with you both this afternoon.

B

Examples

Come in and sit down.   Do come in and sit down.
Have a cigarette.   Do have a cigarette.

Make yourself comfortable.
Have another drink.
Ask for any help you need.
Make yourself at home.

C

Examples

There's a lot to learn at first.   I suppose there is.
We have a lot of work to do.   I suppose you have.

The Marketing Department is very busy.
Ruth has a lot of letters to type.
Everything is so new and strange.
We're all very busy.
Mr Green works very hard.

D

Examples

There's so much to learn at first.	There certainly is!
The Sales Department is so busy!	It certainly is!

You have so much work to do!
You all look so busy!
Mrs Wood is a very attractive woman!
Ruth is a very efficient secretary!
Discovery Engineering is a very go-ahead company!

Comprehension

1. When do all management trainees have to go and see the Personnel Manager?
2. What welfare services does he tell them about?
3. What does he give them?
4. What does the booklet contain?
5. When will Sheila and David be eligible to join the pension and life assurance schemes?
6. How does one go about joining the sports and social club?
7. What about the voluntary savings scheme?
8. What else would David like to know?
9. Who will give him this information?
10. Have Sheila and David enjoyed their first week at Discovery Engineering?
11. Do you think Discovery Engineering is a good firm to work for? Why?
12. What can we learn about Sheila and David from their questions to Mr Mather?

10 Review of the Week

Introduction

On Friday afternoon, Mr Green's secretary telephones David to say that Mr Green is on his way to see Mr Blake. While he is in the Marketing Department he would like to have a chat with Sheila and David. David tells Mrs Wood where he is going and then makes his way over to the Marketing Department. While he is chatting to Sheila, Mr Green arrives; a moment or two later Mr Blake comes along and they all go into the latter's office. They discuss their experiences during their first week and Mr Green explains the next stage of the training programme.

Dialogue

BLAKE: Ah, you're all here! Good—let's go into my office. Sit down everyone and make yourselves comfortable. Do smoke if you want to.

ALL: Thank you.

BLAKE: Now, Mr Green, you're wondering no doubt how your two newcomers have been getting along. We'll let them tell us how they feel about things, shall we? You first, Miss Smith.

SHEILA: Well, I feel a bit bewildered, of course. There's so much to learn. But I think I have a fairly clear picture of the sales set-up. I know we have a network of distributors who hold stocks of our products and supply the smaller users. Big orders are fulfilled directly from the factory here.

BLAKE: That's right. The country is divided into four regions: London and the Home Counties; Wales and the West of England; Scotland, Northern Ireland and the North-West; and finally, the Midlands, North-East England and East Anglia.

DAVID: How many salesmen have we?

BLAKE: We have a sales force at present of twenty-four salesmen on the road, each with his own territory. In addition, every region has a local manager who supervises the region and runs the regional office.

DAVID: How many different products do we make?

BLAKE: There are at present about fifteen basic products but there are several different types and sizes of each. Just lately, R & D have been very active and there are a number of new products in the pipeline. You've heard of BI99 of course?

DAVID: Yes, I've been doing some work on that.

BLAKE: We hope to launch it before the end of the year. And we're

about to embark on a preliminary evaluation of another idea which R & D are very excited about.
SHEILA: Excuse me, what does *R & D* stand for?
BLAKE: It stands for *Research and Development*; it's a department within the organization which carries out research and develops new products.
DAVID: What does a preliminary evaluation involve?
GREEN: That's what you are both going to find out next week. There's going to be a meeting in my office on Tuesday morning at 10.30. I'd like you both to sit in. If we decide to go ahead with the new product, you'll be able to follow all the stages of its development.
BLAKE: Well, it's nearly 5.30—time to be off! Have a nice week-end everyone!
ALL: Thank you. Same to you! etc.

Lesson Notes

David makes his way over to the Marketing Department = David goes to the Marketing Department.
Let's ask them to tell us how they feel about things. Things is here used in an indefinite, impersonal way to include all aspects of the matter under consideration. *How are things with you?* is an equivalent question to *How are you getting on?* and calls for a reply giving family, business or personal details, depending on the circumstances under which the question is asked.
What does R & D stand for? This is the normal way of asking the meaning of initials or other abbreviations.
to sit in at a meeting = to attend as an observer without playing an active part
Does Mr Blake mind . . . ? (see Comprehension questions) This is an alternative to: *Does Mr Blake object to . . . ?* We often use this expression when making polite requests. Examples: *Do you mind if I open a window?* instead of: *May I open a window? Do you mind opening the window?* instead of: *Will you please open the window?*

Drills

A

comfortable.   make yourselves comfortable.
everyone   Sit down, everyone
Sit down, everyone and make yourselves comfortable.

shall we?   feel about things, shall we?   tell us how they feel about things, shall we?
We'll let them tell us how they feel about things, shall we?

sales set-up.   picture of the sales set-up.   a fairly clear picture of the sales set-up.
I think I have a fairly clear picture of the sales set-up.

in the pipeline.   new products in the pipeline.   a number of new products in the pipeline.   there are a number of new products in the pipeline.

very active   R & D have been very active   Just lately, R & D have been very active
Just lately, R & D have been very active and there are a number of new products in the pipeline.

another idea.   evaluation of another idea.   preliminary evaluation of another idea.
embark on a preliminary evaluation of another idea.
We're about to embark on a preliminary evaluation of another idea.

involve?   evaluation involve?   preliminary evaluation involve?
What does a preliminary evaluation involve?

everyone!   week-end, everyone!   nice week-end, everyone!
Have a nice week-end, everyone!

B

Examples

We're running a management training scheme.	What does a management training scheme involve?
We're planning a new advertising campaign.	What does a new advertising campaign involve?

We're embarking on a product evaluation.
We're setting up a network of distributors.
We're organizing a sales convention.
We're conducting a market survey.

C

Examples

Don't discuss it outside the office.	You mustn't discuss it outside the office.
Tell the printers at once.	You must tell the printers at once.

Don't forget the performance data.
Order some new brochures.
Don't move the desk.
Do the filing to-day.

D

Examples
You mustn't discuss it outside the office.	It mustn't be discussed outside the office.
You must tell the printers at once.	The printers must be told at once.

You mustn't forget the performance data.
You must order some new brochures.
You mustn't move the desk.
You must do the filing to-day.

E

Examples
R & D	What does R & D stand for?
It stands for Research & Development.	
BBC	What does BBC stand for?
It stands for British Broadcasting Corporation.	
IBA	What does IBA stand for?
It stands for Independent Broadcasting Authority.	

CBI
It stands for Confederation of British Industry.
ECGD
It stands for Export Credits Guarantee Department.
LOB
It stands for Location of Offices Bureau.
MP
It stands for Member of Parliament.

Comprehension

1. Why does Mr Green want to have a chat with Sheila and David?
2. Is it a formal or an informal meeting? How do we know this?
3. Does Mr Blake mind if people smoke in his office?
4. What do you understand by a network of distributors?

5 How does Sheila feel after her first week?
6 Does she understand the sales organization of the company?
7 Into what regions is the country divided for sales purposes?
8 What users are supplied by the distributors?
9 How are different sizes of orders handled?
10 Why are R & D so excited?
11 What does R & D stand for?
12 What is the function of R & D?
13 Why is there going to be a meeting next week?
14 Where will the meeting take place?

11 The Draft Brochure

Introduction

On Monday morning Mrs Wood asks David how he is getting on with the draft of the BI99 brochure. He shows her what he has done so far and they discuss his ideas. Mrs Wood makes some suggestions and points out some items he has left out. During the conversation, David mentions the product evaluation meeting to which he and Sheila have been invited. Mrs Wood explains the term *product evaluation* and some other expressions likely to be used at the forthcoming meeting. She tells him that she knows about the product to be evaluated but that the Advertising Section is not involved at this stage.

Dialogue

MRS WOOD: Good morning, David. Did you have a nice week-end?
DAVID: Good morning, Mrs Wood. Very nice thanks. Did you?
MRS WOOD: Not bad at all, thank you. We went for a walk on Sunday afternoon. The countryside looks lovely at this time of year.
DAVID: Yes, there's some very pretty country round here, isn't there?
MRS WOOD: You don't come from this part of the world, do you?
DAVID: No, my home's in Surrey. But I like it here in the Midlands very much.
MRS WOOD: That's good. Well now, back to work! How's the BI99 job coming along?
DAVID: Here's what I've done so far. Would you care to glance through it?
MRS WOOD: Let's go through it together, shall we? Now, let's see... revolutionary new design... simple to install and operate ... cut your production costs... reduce staff fatigue... that last one's a bit far-fetched, isn't it? We mustn't make exaggerated claims, must we?
DAVID: No, I suppose not. Perhaps I'd better take that out.
MRS WOOD: Yes, I think so. Now, where are you going to put the performance data?
DAVID: Oh dear, I haven't left a space for that.

MRS WOOD: Never mind, we can make room for it. We must also leave a space for the name and address of the company and a list of the area offices. And don't forget the words *patents pending*.
DAVID: Shall I rearrange the lay-out?
MRS WOOD: Yes—and then ask the visualizer to do a mock-up, please.
DAVID: Right. By the way, do you know Mr Green has invited Sheila and me to a meeting to-morrow?
MRS WOOD: Ah yes, the product evaluation meeting. I shan't be there—the Advertising Section isn't involved at this stage.
DAVID: I'm not sure I understand what *product evaluation* means.
MRS WOOD: Very simply, it's an attempt to decide whether a product is likely to be a good thing for the company to make. Will it give a good return on the money it will cost to develop it? What is the market potential? How fierce is the competition? How long will it take to break even?
DAVID: What does *break even* mean?
MRS WOOD: When we have recovered the original cost of developing and launching a product, we say it has *broken even* or reached *break-even point*. This may take several years. Some people call this the *pay-back* period.
DAVID: Who decides if a product is worth developing?
MRS WOOD: We have a product committee; it consists of Mr Blake and Mr Green, the Manufacturing Director and the Financial Director. They decide whether to drop the product, whether to carry out further research and development, or whether to refer it to a meeting of the full Board.

Lesson Notes

isn't there? and *do you?* are examples of question tags. This idiomatic form is dealt with in detail in grammar note 47.
How's the BI99 job coming along? = What progress are you making . . .? Compare this with *How are you getting on with . . .?*
to glance through = to read quickly through (a draft etc.) but not in detail
to go through = to read or examine more thoroughly
far-fetched = highly unlikely, improbable
a mock-up = a sketch, design or model which gives a visual impression of the final result. Compare this with *visual* in Episode 4.
The advertising section is not involved at this stage = the advertising section does not yet have any part in the matter.
to drop = to discontinue (a project)

Grammar

The main points introduced in this Episode are:
46   Using the simple past tense
47   The question tag
48   *Had better*
49   *ago*

Drills

A

Good morning, David.
a nice week-end?   have a nice week-end?
Good morning, David.   Did you have a nice week-end?

Good morning, Mrs Wood.   Very nice thanks.   Did you?
thank you.   at all, thank you.   Not bad at all, thank you.

coming along?   the BI99 job coming along?   How's the BI99 job coming along?

so far.   done so far.   what I've done so far.
Here's what I've done so far.

through it?   glance through it?   care to glance through it?
Would you care to glance through it?

must we?   exaggerated claims, must we?   make exaggerated claims, must we?
We mustn't make exaggerated claims, must we?

take that out   better take that out   Perhaps I'd better take that out
No, I suppose not. Perhaps I'd better take that out.

B

Examples

How are you getting on with the brochure? (finish/nearly)   I've nearly finished it.

How's the report coming along? (start/only just)   I've only just started it.

When will the mock-up be ready? (start/not yet)

How is David getting on with the brochure? (finish/nearly)
How is Mrs Wood getting on with her report? (start/only just)
How are you getting on with this drill? (finish/nearly)

C

Examples

Has David finished the brochure? (yesterday)	Yes, he finished it yesterday.
Has he telephoned the printers? (this morning)	Yes, he telephoned them this morning.

Has Mr Green interviewed the trainees? (last week)
Have the proofs arrived? (half an hour ago)
Has the post come? (ten minutes ago)
Have you done the filing? (before lunch)

D

Examples

There's going to be a product evaluation meeting.	What does *product evaluation* mean?
We must include the words *patents pending*.	What does *patents pending* mean?

We'll ask the visualizer to do a mock-up.
We have to assess the market potential.
We hope to break even in three years.
We have to assess the pay-back period.

E In this drill, a manager is talking to a trainee. He has made notes of the things he wants to say to him.

Examples

second paragraph—re-write	You'd better re-write the second paragraph.
exaggerated claims—don't make	You'd better not make exaggerated claims.

layout—rearrange
performance data—include
out-of-date statistics—don't quote
old photographs—don't use

Comprehension

1. Did David and Mrs Wood enjoy the week-end?
2. How did Mrs Wood spend Sunday afternoon?
3. Did she go for a walk by herself?
4. What part of the world does David come from?
5. How does he like living in the Midlands?
6. What claims does David make for BI99 in his draft brochure?
7. Does Mrs Wood approve of his draft?
8. What alterations must he make?
9. What has he left out?
10. How can he make room for the items he has forgotten?
11. What will he ask the visualizer to do?
12. What does Mrs Wood tell David about the product evaluation meeting?
13. Will Mrs Wood be at the meeting?
14. Why not?

12 Some Aspects of Selling and Marketing

Introduction

While David is having his discussion with Mrs Wood, Sheila is questioning Mr Blake on some aspects of selling and marketing. She asks how the salesmen are recruited, what qualifications they need and whether the company runs training schemes. Mr Blake explains that the company looks for young men with a good all-round education and a good personality. Some experience of selling is always useful but the company runs its own training schemes, including product training. Technical qualifications are not essential but are, of course, very useful. The regional managers all have some technical qualifications and they can always consult one of the project or design engineers if they need help.

Dialogue

SHEILA: Mr Blake, may I ask you a few questions, please?
BLAKE: Of course, Sheila—you don't mind my calling you by your first name, do you?
SHEILA: Please do.
BLAKE: What do you want to know?
SHEILA: First of all, how do we start selling a new product? Do the salesmen just walk into the customers' premises and say: 'Here's a wonderful new something-or-other to solve all your problems'?
BLAKE: Well, in some cases they may do just that! But a great deal of work has been done beforehand in the way of product development, market research, test marketing and so on.
SHEILA: How is market research carried out?
BLAKE: That's a very wide question indeed. Whole books are written on the subject. But one of the objects of market research is to find out whether there is a market for the product and whether we can sell the product in that market. Sometimes we carry out our own research. For major products where development costs are likely to be high, we employ specialists.
SHEILA: Do our own salesmen take part?
BLAKE: In the early stages, only the regional managers are involved. If we decide to do some test marketing, some of the senior salesmen are brought into the picture.
SHEILA: What do you mean by *test marketing*?
BLAKE: We manufacture a small quantity of the product and

offer it to certain selected customers to find out their reactions. It's a technique we can only use for items which are comparatively cheap and simple to produce.
SHEILA: Are our salesmen specially trained?
BLAKE: We give them all an intensive initial training course when they first join the company; this includes product training.
SHEILA: Product training?
BLAKE: We have to ensure that all our salesmen fully understand the various applications, design features, special advantages and so on of all the products in our range.
SHEILA: Do they receive any further training?
BLAKE: Once a year they undergo a short refresher course.
SHEILA: Well, thank you, Mr Blake. I feel I'll be able to understand to-morrow's meeting much better after the information you've just given me.

Lesson Notes

to run = (in this context) to organize
to carry out (a task, a project) = to perform all the activities necessary to complete it
... *some of the senior salesmen are brought into the picture* = some of the senior salesmen are asked to participate in the project. Compare: to put someone in the picture = to give them background and/or up-to-date information on the subject under discussion.

Grammar
The main points introduced in this Episode are:
50 *may*
51 Possessive before a gerund (the *-ing* form of a verb)

Drills

A

questions, please? a few questions, please? ask you a few questions, please?
May I ask you a few questions, please?

do you? by your first name, do you? mind my calling you by your first name, do you? You don't mind my calling you by your first name, do you?

we employ specialists.
likely to be high, development costs are likely to be high,

Where development costs are likely to be high,
Where development costs are likely to be high, we employ specialists.

into the picture.　brought into the picture.　senior salesmen are brought into the picture.　some of the senior salesmen are brought into the picture.

test marketing,　decide to do some test marketing,　if we decide to do some test marketing,
If we decide to do some test marketing, some of the senior salesmen are brought into the picture.

B

Examples

Ask how the salesmen are recruited.	How are the salesmen recruited?
Ask what qualifications they need.	What qualifications do they need?

Ask if they receive any further training.
Ask how many salesmen we have.
Ask how many products there are.
Ask how we start selling a product.
Ask what test marketing means.
Ask if the regional managers are technically qualified.
Ask how many sales regions there are.

C

Examples

sell new product?	How do we set about selling a new product?
produce new brochure?	How do we set about producing a new brochure?

recruit salesmen?
train managers?
increase turnover?
reduce costs?
improve staff relations?
reduce absenteeism?

Comprehension

1. What is Sheila doing in this Episode?
2. Is Mr Blake willing to answer her questions?
3. How are the salesmen trained?
4. What does *product training* mean?
5. If a salesman needs technical help, who can he ask?
6. If a regional manager needs technical help, who can he ask?
7. Does Discovery Engineering carry out its own market research?
8. How is test marketing carried out?
9. What are its limitations?
10. What kind of work must be done before a new product is launched?
11. Do the salesmen have to be qualified?
12. Why are education and personality more important than selling experience?
13. What qualities does the company look for when recruiting salesmen?
14. What qualifications do the regional managers need?
15. In what way does Sheila feel that her conversation with Mr Blake has been useful?

13 The Product Evaluation Meeting—One

Introduction

When David and Sheila arrive at Mr Green's office on Tuesday morning, they find him talking to two men whom they have not met before. Mr Green introduces them—Mr Pound, the Manufacturing Director, and the Financial Director, Mr Miles, who is also the Company Secretary.

A new product has been developed by the engineers in R & D. The idea was born when a customer, Jones Electronics Ltd, asked for help with a technical problem on their production line. R & D designed a device which proved very effective, and some people now want it added to the company's standard range of products.

Dialogue

GREEN: Well, gentlemen, as you know the purpose of this meeting is to make a preliminary evaluation of product CP21. At this stage we have three main points to consider—you have them on your agenda. The first one is: potential market. Tom, what can you say about that?

BLAKE: I asked the four regional managers to do two things. Firstly, to make a rough estimate of the number of customers in their territory who might be interested and secondly, to sound out one or two of these—very diplomatically of course—and find out their reactions. Basically, I wanted to know whether this problem is a general one or not.

GREEN: And what were their findings?

BLAKE: Well, it seems the problem is more general than we realized. But most people just accept it—they regard it more as an inconvenience than as a serious production problem.

GREEN: Do you think the idea has sales potential?

BLAKE: Yes, I do. The results obtained by Jones Electronics are quite impressive.

GREEN: Thank you. Now, the next item to consider is the probable cost of going into production. Bill, can you give us some idea of the investment required?

POUND: The product is basically fairly simple, and no unfamiliar technology is involved. Tooling-up would not be too expensive and we have factory space available. Some components would have to be bought in and we should have to recruit some skilled labour for the machine operations and semi-skilled workers for the assembly. I've jotted down some figures; here they are.

GREEN: Thank you, that's a great help. That brings us to our third point: financial evaluation. Stephen, may we have your comments?
MILES: I see you hope to break even in under three years. That's very optimistic, isn't it?
POUND: Well, Tom gave me some very optimistic reports from his regional sales managers.
BLAKE: I'm sure the potential is there, but it's quite a new concept and it may take time to persuade people to accept it. The initial cost to a customer of adapting his production line may seem to him to be quite high. It will be our job to convince him that it will be a sound investment.
GREEN: I can see we shall have to go into all this a bit more thoroughly. Let's break off for a cup of coffee.
ALL: Good idea!

Lesson Notes

To sound out = to make discreet enquiries
I've jotted down some figures = I've made brief notes of some figures.
to jot down = to make a written note for one's own personal use or for information. Such a note is sometimes used later as the basis of a more detailed report.
I'm sure the potential is there = I'm sure the potential exists.
They regard it more as an inconvenience than as a serious production problem. Here *more* is being used to mean *rather*. The sentence could be rephrased to read: *They do not regard it as a serious production problem, but rather as an inconvenience.*

Grammar

The main points introduced in this Episode are:
52 Conditional forms
53 Reported speech

Drills

A

CP21.   product CP21.   a preliminary evaluation of product CP21.
to make a preliminary evaluation of product CP21.

this meeting   the purpose of this meeting   as you know, the purpose of this meeting
Well gentlemen, as you know, the purpose of this meeting
Well gentlemen, as you know, the purpose of this meeting is to make a preliminary evaluation of product CP21.

a general one or not. whether this problem is a general one or not.
I want to know whether this problem is a general one or not.

investment required?   An idea of the investment required?
Can you give us an idea of the investment required?

optimistic, isn't it? very optimistic, isn't it?
That's very optimistic, isn't it?

under three years. break even in under three years.
I see you hope to break even in under three years.
I see you hope to break even in under three years. That's very optimistic, isn't it?

B As chairman of an informal meeting, you invite your colleagues to accept your suggestions as the meeting proceeds.

Examples

get down to business	Let's get down to business, shall we?
move on to the next item	Let's move on to the next item, shall we?

look more closely at the figures
ask the Company Secretary for his views
break off for a cup of coffee
meet here at the same time next week
adjourn for lunch

C You have made some notes about a project, and are explaining them to a colleague.
You are in favour of the project but you have some reservations.

Examples

design good/too expensive?	I'm sure the design is good, but it may be too expensive.
product sound/Board reject?	I'm sure the product is sound, but the Board may reject it.

can solve problems/take time?
can increase productivity/unions object?
can change design/take too long?
money available/interest too high?
Can make product/need more workers?

D Now you are discussing the project with your colleague. You still have your reservations.

Examples

Can we solve the problems, do you think? (take time)	Yes, we can solve the problems, but it'll take time.
Is the design good, do you think? (too expensive)	Yes, the design's good, but it'll be too expensive.

Can we increase productivity, do you think? (unions object)
Can we change the design, do you think? (take too long)
Can we raise the money, do you think? (interest too high)
Is the product sound, do you think? (Board reject)
Can we make the product, do you think? (need more workers)

Comprehension

1 How did product CP21 originate?
2 What does the term *potential market* mean?
3 What did Mr Blake instruct his regional managers to do?
4 What did he want them to find out?
5 What were their findings?
6 What is Mr Blake's opinion of the product's potential?
7 What grounds has he for this opinion?
8 Does Mr Pound consider that CP21 would be difficult to manufacture? Why not?
9 Is he in favour of the product?
10 What would the labour requirements be?
11 What about factory space?
12 What is Mr Miles' attitude to CP21?

14 The Product Evaluation Meeting—Two

Introduction

Over coffee, David and Sheila have the opportunity of chatting to the two Directors whom they have just met. David is interested in the system of coding used for new products and Mr Pound explains that BI stands for *Bright Idea*. All products developed as the result of an idea from someone within the company are given BI numbers. A product which is developed in response to a customer's request for help is given a CP number—*Customer Problem*.

Mr Miles explains that in addition to controlling the financial aspect of the new product, he is responsible—as Company Secretary—for arranging patent protection both in England and overseas. If any manufacturing licences are negotiated it will be his job to prepare the necessary documents.

Dialogue

GREEN: Now, let's resume our discussion. Stephen, are you prepared at this stage to make a financial evaluation? Do you think we're justified in spending money on further development of CP21?

MILES: I don't think we've done enough research. We know that Jones Electronics had a problem; we solved that problem with CP21. We know that some other people have the same problem but that they think of it as an inconvenience rather than a problem. Now, how do we know that CP21 will work for everyone?

POUND: I'm prepared to state that CP21 can be adapted to give good results over a very wide range of engineering processes. Of course, some production methods will show better results than others.

MILES: All right. But can we get people to take the problem seriously? Can we convince them that CP21 will solve it for them? Can we persuade them that the results will justify the initial investment?

GREEN: Those are very sound questions. Tom, can you suggest some lines for further market research?

BLAKE: Well, we could talk to some selected customers and show them a prototype. We could even ask Jones Electronics for permission to quote some of their improved production figures.

MILES: I know what all that means—more items on the expense account!

GREEN: Well, well—that's all part and parcel of marketing, isn't it? What about the question of a prototype, Bill? Does that present any problems?
POUND: Not that I can think of. Of course, some design modifications might be needed in specific cases, but the basic principle would remain the same. Do you want me to go ahead with a prototype, then?
GREEN: Tom?
BLAKE: Yes, please. How soon can you let us have it?
POUND: It shouldn't take more than two or three weeks at the outside.
BLAKE: Fine. There's one other point I want to make. Our preliminary research only covered existing users of our products. I believe there is an even larger potential among non-users. If we can open new accounts with CP21 we may get new customers for our other products.
MILES: That would certainly be a point in its favour! It would go a long way to improving cost-effectiveness. By the way, we have of course arranged patent protection.
GREEN: Good. Well, I think that's all for now. Tom, will you let me know when you're ready for a further meeting?
BLAKE: Yes, thanks, I will.
GREEN: Right. Now, is there any other business?
ALL: No. That's it, I think.
GREEN: In that case I declare the meeting closed.

Lesson Notes

Can we get people to take the problem seriously? =Can we persuade them to take it seriously?
To get someone to do something means to cause them to do it by asking, persuading, or instructing them to do it.
Examples:
I'll get my secretary to type that=I'll instruct, tell her to type it.
I'll get my wife to meet us with the car=I'll ask her to meet us.
That's all part and parcel of marketing=that's one of the normal activities associated with marketing.
to go ahead=to proceed (i.e. with a project)
at the outside=at the most

Drills

A

CP21?   further development of CP21?
spending money   justified in spending money   Do you think we're justified in spending money

Do you think we're justified in spending money on further development of CP21?

than others.   better results than others.   will show better results than others.
Of course, some production methods will show better results than others.

initial investment?   justify the initial investment?   the results will justify the initial investment?   Can we persuade them that the results will justify the initial investment?

new accounts with CP21   if we can open new accounts with CP21
our other products.   new customers for our other products.   we may get new customers for our other products.
If we can open new accounts with CP21, we may get new customers for our other products.

its favour!   point in its favour!   certainly be a point in its favour!
That would certainly be a point in its favour!

B

Examples

Are we going to launch the product or drop it?	The Board will decide whether to launch the product or whether to drop it.
Are we going to accept the report or reject it?	The Board will decide whether to accept the report or whether to reject it.

Are we going to maintain the patent or allow it to lapse?
Are we going to sell abroad or concentrate on the home market?
Are we going to build a canteen or give Luncheon Vouchers?
Are we going to move to new premises or expand the existing ones?

C

Examples

Would you have to recruit more labour?	Yes, if we decided to go ahead, we'd have to recruit more labour.
Would you need to train more salesmen?	Yes, if we decided to go ahead, we'd need to train more salesmen.

Would you have to find more storage space?
Would you need more office staff?
Would you need more skilled men?
Would you need to do more advertising?
Would you need to raise more money?

D

Examples

We're going to need more labour.	Will you let me know when you're going to need more labour?
We're going to need more salesmen.	Will you let me know when you're going to need more salesmen?

We're going to need more storage space.
We're going to need more office staff.
We're going to need more skilled men.
We're going to need a further meeting.

Comprehension

1. What does BI stand for?
2. What does CP stand for?
3. What is the meaning of the two codes?
4. Who controls the financial aspect of a new product?
5. What other matters is he responsible for?
6. Why isn't Mr Miles in favour of CP21?

7 What questions does he ask?
8 Who does Mr Green refer these questions to?
9 What suggestions does Mr Blake offer?
10 Are there any objections to his ideas?
11 Does Mr Pound have confidence in CP21?
12 How does he qualify his opinion?
13 What further possible argument in favour of CP21 does Mr Blake put forward?
14 How does Mr Miles react to this?
15 When will the next meeting of the Product Committee be held?

15 Cost-Effectiveness in Business

Introduction

After the product evaluation meeting, Mr Green shows Sheila and David the Product Sheet which is being used to record the progress of CP21. He tells them that Mr Pound, the Manufacturing Director, will appoint one of his team to be *Product Manager* for CP21. The Product Manager will be responsible for co-ordinating all the activities necessary to the development of the product, such as the ordering of materials and components, allocation of factory and storage space, preparation of advertising material, costing and pricing, and so on. The trainees are puzzled by the term *cost-effectiveness* used by both Mr Miles and Mr Green.

Dialogue

GREEN: Well, what did you make of all that?
DAVID: I'm just beginning to realize how little I know about industry!
SHEILA: So am I!
GREEN: Oh, you mustn't feel disheartened. Things will start to fall into place much sooner than you expect. Now, as you've just heard, we're going to make a prototype CP21 and do some test marketing. We shall appoint a Product Manager; he will be responsible for seeing that all the activities involved in developing the product are properly co-ordinated.
DAVID: There seem to be an awful lot of activities involved—costing, buying, stock control, tool design and so on.
GREEN: Yes. The Product Manager has to liaise with people in all those areas during the entire life cycle of the product.
SHEILA: It all looks very complicated.
GREEN: Running a company is a complicated business nowadays! Every aspect has to be carefully controlled, to ensure maximum cost-effectiveness.
DAVID: Mr Miles used that expression, but I didn't quite understand it.
SHEILA: Neither did I.
GREEN: *Cost-effectiveness*, you mean? Well, let's assume that every activity contributes in some way to the cost of running the company. At the same time, it contributes in some way to the company's revenue. For example, to employ a salesman costs, say £X a day: every time he takes an order he is contributing something to revenue. Now, suppose one

salesman spends all day negotiating one order for £1,000-worth of goods. Another spends the day collecting a number of smaller orders which total the same sum. Which of the two salesmen is the more cost-effective?

DAVID: They're both the same, surely. I mean, they've both done a thousand pounds'-worth of business in the day.

GREEN: No, they're not. An order worth £100 costs just as much to process as one for £1,000; it has to be confirmed, passed to the stores, checked, packed, despatched, invoiced and so on. So the one order for £1,000 is worth more in terms of real profit than, say, ten orders for £100 each.

SHEILA: I'm beginning to understand. But surely, some activities don't bring in any revenue at all—telephone calls, for example?

GREEN: Can you imagine running a business without a telephone? Other charges would soar—postage, stationery, typists' wages and so on. You'd lose a lot of business because of a fall in efficiency. But you're right up to a point—some telephone calls are a complete waste of money. We try to encourage everyone to use the phone as efficiently as possible. Now, let's take a closer look at this product sheet.

Lesson Notes

Things will start to fall into place = You will begin to understand more clearly.
an awful lot of activities = a great many activities
Overheads—this is a term which includes all the costs (other than manufacturing costs) which are necessary for the running of a business.

Grammar

The main point introduced in this Episode is:
54 *seem to be, may be*

Drills

A

heard, you've just heard, now, as you've just heard,
test marketing. do some test marketing.
prototype CP21 make a prototype CP21 we're going to make a prototype CP21
Now, as you've just heard, we're going to make a prototype CP21
Now, as you've just heard, we're going to make a prototype CP21 and do some test marketing.

cost-effectiveness.   maximum cost-effectiveness.   to ensure maximum cost-effectiveness.
carefully controlled   has to be carefully controlled   every aspect has to be carefully controlled
Every aspect has to be carefully controlled to ensure maximum cost-effectiveness.

understand it.   quite understand it.   I didn't quite understand it.
expression   that expression   Mr Miles used that expression
Mr Miles used that expression but I didn't quite understand it.

B

Examples

I don't quite understand what cost-effectiveness means.	Neither do I.
I thought the meeting was very interesting.	So did I.

I didn't understand everything, though.
I hope Mr Green will explain things to us.
I didn't take any notes at the meeting.
I wasn't bored during the meeting.
But I was rather disheartened.
I'm not going to the next meeting.
I'm beginning to feel hungry!
Let's go to lunch, shall we!

C

Examples

Costing's the same as buying, isn't it?	No, it's not.
A telephone isn't essential to a business, is it?	Yes, it is.
All salesmen are efficient, aren't they?	No, they're not.

The salesmen are all qualified, aren't they?
The regional managers aren't qualified, are they?
Marketing's the same as selling, isn't it?
A car isn't essential for a salesman, is it?

Mr Green isn't a Director, is he?
David's a Product Manager, isn't he?
Mrs Wood works in R & D,
doesn't she?
Sheila doesn't like David, does she?

D Your colleague is giving you some interesting information. You are surprised and impressed, and you show this by the tone of your voice as well as by your replies.

Examples

I've done business to-day worth £10,000.	You mean you've done ten thousand pounds'-worth of business?
I've sold cars this week worth £100,000.	You mean you've sold a hundred thousand pounds'-worth of cars?

I've ordered goods this morning worth £500.
Because of sickness, I've lost orders this month worth £20,000.
We'll need new equipment costing £200,000.
The Chairman has given his wife jewellery worth £25,000.

Comprehension

1 How is the progress of a new product recorded at Discovery Engineering?
2 Name some of the activities necessary to the development of a new product.
3 Can you add to the list given in the text?
4 Who will be appointed to look after CP21?
5 What will be his chief responsibility?
6 How does Mr Green explain the term *cost-effectiveness*?
7 Do you think his explanation is a good one?
8 Can you give an alternative explanation?
9 What activities are involved in the processing of an order?
10 Is it true to say that telephone calls do not bring in any revenue at all?
11 What are the principal overheads of a manufacturing company?
12 What items would you include under the heading *manufacturing costs*?

16 The Product Manager is Appointed

Introduction

For every new product under active consideration at Discovery Engineering a Product Manager is appointed. His first task is to assemble all the information necessary to enable the directors of the company to decide whether to invest in the product. The headings under which information has to be obtained are set out on a product sheet.

While Mr Green is explaining this to Sheila and David, Mr Pound rings through to say that John Edwards has been appointed Product Manager for CP21. John has been with Discovery for nearly two years; he began as a trainee, like Sheila and David, and started work in the Production Department some months ago after his initial one-year training period. CP21 is his first assignment. Mr Green suggests that Sheila and David arrange to visit the factory in the near future, to meet John and learn more about the function of a Product Manager.

Dialogue

GREEN: As you see, the product sheet is really a summary or check-list of everything we need to know when we are considering a new product. Information under all these headings will be collected by the Product Manager, who will then prepare a detailed report. This will be considered by a further meeting of the Product Committee, who will decide whether or not to recommend the product to the Board.
SHEILA: Who makes the final decision?
GREEN: The Board of Directors.
DAVID: How many Directors are there?
GREEN: Seven. Mr Blake, Mr Pound and Mr Miles you have already met. Mr Young is the Overseas Director, Mr Browning is the Chairman and Managing Director and Mr Simpson is a non-executive Director. I am Management Services Director. (*The telephone rings*) Excuse me... Green!
POUND: Bill Pound here. We've put John Edwards in charge of CP21. You remember him, don't you? He's one of the last intake of trainees. He's been in my department since last May.
GREEN: Oh yes, I remember him. I thought he was a promising chap. Is this his first assignment?
POUND: Yes. It seemed like a suitable one for him to cut his teeth on.

GREEN: Perhaps my two new trainees can come over and see him some time, and get some first-hand information about the job.
POUND: By all means! There's nothing like explaining a job to someone else for getting it straight in your own mind!
GREEN: Thanks. I'll tell them to give him a ring and fix a date. Is that all for now?
POUND: Yes, I think so.
GREEN: OK then. Good-bye.
POUND: Good-bye.
GREEN: (*Hangs up*) That was Mr Pound. John Edwards has been made Product Manager for CP21. He started as a management trainee like yourselves—it must be getting on for a couple of years ago. I expect you've gathered that I've suggested you go over to have a chat with him. Mr Pound is quite agreeable.
DAVID: When shall we go?
GREEN: Any time that's convenient for all concerned. Naturally, you'll have to check with Mrs Wood and Mr Blake first. It might be as well to wait for a couple of days—that will give John time to make a start on his assignment.
SHEILA: I take it we are to continue in our present departments for the time being?
GREEN: Oh yes. There's going to be plenty going on in Marketing during the coming weeks—we've got a sales convention coming up shortly.
DAVID: I believe Mrs Wood mentioned that we're exhibiting at a trade fair later this year.
GREEN: That's right. You'll soon find out there's never a dull moment with Discovery Engineering!

Lesson Notes

to ring through = to call on the internal telephone
It seemed like a suitable one for him to cut his teeth on = It seemed suitable for his first assignment as Product Manager.
to give someone a ring = to call them on the telephone
getting on for = nearly
I expect you've gathered = I expect you have deduced or understood (from what I said)
Mr Pound is quite agreeable = Mr Pound agrees with the suggestion.
It might be as well is a form of words introducing a piece of advice.
There's going to be plenty going on = A number of different things are going to happen; there are going to be a lot of activities taking place.

Grammar

The main point introduced in this Episode is:
55 *for* and *since* in expressions of time

Drills

A

in your own mind.   straight in your own mind.   for getting it straight in your own mind.
to someone else   explaining a job to someone else   There's nothing like explaining a job to someone else
There's nothing like explaining a job to someone else for getting it straight in your own mind.

start on his assignment.   time to start on his assignment.   that will give John time to start on his assignment.
a couple of days   as well to wait for a couple of days   It might be as well to wait for a couple of days
It might be as well to wait for a couple of days—that will give John time to start on his assignment.

coming up shortly.   a sales convention coming up shortly.   we've got a sales convention coming up shortly.
during the coming weeks   in Marketing during the coming weeks   plenty going on in Marketing during the coming weeks
There's going to be plenty going on in Marketing during the coming weeks
There's going to be plenty going on in Marketing during the coming weeks—we've got a sales convention coming up shortly.

B

Examples

Explaining a job to someone else helps you to get it straight in your own mind.	There's nothing like explaining a job to someone else for getting it straight in your own mind.
Visiting England will improve your English.	There's nothing like visiting England for improving your English.

If you join a social club, you'll meet new people.
The best way to see the countryside is to walk.

Talking to a colleague often helps to solve a problem.
If you want to keep fit, play golf.
You must advertise if you want to improve your sales figures.

C

Examples

I want to see John Edwards. (wait for a couple of days)

If you want to see John Edwards, it might be as well to wait for a couple of days.

I must talk to the Chairman. (have a word with his secretary)

If you want to talk to the Chairman, it might be as well to have a word with his secretary.

I'd like to visit the factory. (ask the Manufacturing Director)
I'll go and see the buyer. (make an appointment first)
I'd like to take the day off. (ask your supervisor)
When can I visit the regional office? (telephone the regional manager)

Comprehension

1. Who is to be the Product Manager for CP21?
2. How long has he been with the company?
3. How long is the initial training period for management trainees?
4. How many other assignments has John Edwards had?
5. How will he set about his task?
6. What is Mr Green's opinion of John Edwards?
7. What does Mr Green suggest to Mr Pound? Why?
8. What is Mr Pound's reaction? Why?
9. How will the visit be arranged?
10. What does Mr Green tell David and Sheila to do before visiting John? Why?
11. What future events are mentioned in the conversation?
12. How will the final decision about CP21 be taken?

17 A Visit to the Works—One

Introduction

Following Mr Green's suggestion, Sheila and David arrange to go over to the factory to meet John Edwards. John is 26; he joined Discovery nearly two years ago as a management trainee. After one year with the company he was offered a choice between the Production and Marketing Departments, and he chose the former. Before going into details about his assignment as Product Manager for CP21 he gives Sheila and David some background information on the organization of the factory.

Dialogue

JOHN: Hullo—come in! I'm John Edwards.
DAVID: Hullo, John. I'm David Long and this is Sheila Smith.
SHEILA: How do you do!
JOHN: Glad to meet you both. Do sit down. When did you join the Company?
DAVID: A week ago last Monday.
JOHN: And where are you working?
DAVID: I'm in Advertising and Sheila's in Marketing.
JOHN: That's where I started—in Marketing, I mean. They offered me a job in one of the Sales Regions after I'd finished my training, but I'm no salesman. Anyway, I believe you're interested in CP21?
DAVID: We sat in at the product evaluation meeting at the beginning of the week. I'm afraid we were both a bit out of our depth.
JOHN: I know the feeling! Perhaps I'd better explain a bit about the set-up here in the factory before we go any further.
SHEILA: That'd be very helpful.
JOHN: As you know, this is the Production Department. Mr Pound is the Manufacturing Director; he's responsible for all aspects of manufacture, from setting up the production line to the moment when the finished article is ready for inspection and testing. He's also responsible for the organization of the whole factory, including despatch and transport. But a lot of other activities are involved in producing the goods and getting them to the customer.
DAVID: And your job is to make sure that all these services are properly co-ordinated?

JOHN: I'm not so important as all that! My terms of reference are simply to keep track of my own product. Overall responsibility for the whole organization lies with the Product Committee. Now, every product the Company makes is the responsibility of someone acting as Product Manager.

SHEILA: Is there a separate product manager for each product?

JOHN: Oh no—there are only three others besides myself. I've just been promoted; CP21 is my first baby.

DAVID: How do you set about the job?

JOHN: By starting a product sheet and going through the checklist of items. You've seen one of these sheets, haven't you?

SHEILA: Yes, Mr Green showed us one.

JOHN: Well now, we're going to make a prototype and do some test marketing. Only small quantities of materials and components will be required for this, but meanwhile I shall be asking our Buying Section to get me some quotations—prices, samples, delivery dates and so forth. Mr Blake and Mr Pound will decide whether to use the original drawings or, make some mods. to the design we produced for Jones Electronics.

SHEILA: What are mods?

JOHN: It's short for modifications. Now, preliminary estimates of manufacturing space, plant and labour requirements have already been made but nothing has been said so far about storage space. We shall need somewhere to store materials, components, finished goods and packaging materials.

DAVID: I see the checklist refers to *bought-in components* and *bought-in products*. What's the difference?

JOHN: *Components* are parts which are incorporated into the finished product. *Bought-in products* are items which are sold with the products but are separate from them. For example, a sewing machine has a motor which is normally bought in by the manufacturer; that is a component. The manufacturer also supplies a tool-kit and a carrying case with each machine. These are separate products which he buys from another manufacturer.

SHEILA: What about packaging?

JOHN: Some products have to be packed individually to prevent damage in transit or because they are normally sold singly anyway. Others are packed in pairs, in dozens or in bulk, depending on their nature. We buy our packaging from specialists who design the containers for us as required. Advertising normally produces a design for the exterior of the container.

DAVID: How do you decide what quantity of a new product to make?

JOHN: I'll answer that one in a moment. Let's have some coffee before we go any further!

Lesson Notes

I'm afraid ... often precedes an admission of some failure or omission on the part of the speaker, and expresses mild regret or apology.
Example: Can you tell me the time? I'm afraid I can't—my watch has stopped.
set-up = organization
I've just been promoted = I am newly promoted. *Just* used with the present perfect tense (or past perfect in reported speech and narrative) implies an action or event in the very recent past.
With the present continuous tense, it implies that one is in the act of doing something. Example: I'm just making a cup of coffee. (action in progress) I've just made a cup of coffee. (action recently completed)
CP21 is my first baby = CP21 is the first product I have been appointed to look after.

Grammar

The main points introduced in this Episode are:
56 *so* ... *as* and *as* ... *as*
57 Past perfect tense

Drills

A

about the set-up   a bit about the set-up   explain a bit about the set-up
Perhaps I'd better explain a bit about the set-up before we go any further.   here in the factory before we go any further.
Perhaps I'd better explain a bit about the set-up here in the factory before we go any further.

already been made,   manufacturing space has already been made,   a preliminary estimate of manufacturing space has already been made,
storage space.   so far about storage space.   nothing has been said so far about storage space.
A preliminary estimate of manufacturing space has been made, but nothing has been said so far about storage space.

packaging materials.   components, finished goods and packaging materials.
somewhere to store materials, components, finished goods and packaging materials.
We shall need somewhere to store materials, components, finished goods and packaging materials.

72

B

Examples

I see you've allocated manufacturing space, but what about storage space?	We haven't allocated storage space yet.
I see you've agreed your plant requirements, but what about labour requirements?	We haven't agreed our labour requirements yet.

I see you've ordered the raw materials, but what about the components?
I see you've allocated a packing area, but what about a loading area?
I see you've finalized the costing, but what about the pricing?
I see you've recruited extra production workers, but what about extra salesmen?

C

Examples

The report refers to *costing* and *pricing*.	What's the difference between *costing* and *pricing*?
It says here: *bought-in goods* and *bought-in components*.	What's the difference between *bought-in goods* and *bought-in components*?

The next item is *Skilled workers and semi-skilled workers*.
There's a reference here to *selling* and *marketing*.
It mentions *flat rates* and *piece rates*
and *wages* and *salaries*.

Comprehension

1 What choice was offered to John Edwards after his first year with Discovery Engineering?
2 When did David and Sheila join the company?

3 Why did John Edwards turn down a job in one of the sales regions?
4 How did David and Sheila feel at the product evaluation meeting?
5 What does John Edwards begin by explaining?
6 What are Mr Pound's responsibilities?
7 What are a Product Manager's terms of reference?
8 Who has overall responsibility for product organization?
9 How many Product Managers are there at present?
10 How will John Edwards set about his job?
11 Will the original drawings be used?
12 What is the difference between a bought-in component and a bought-in product?
13 What considerations affect the way a product is packaged?
14 How are containers for Discovery Engineering's products designed?

18 A Visit to the Works—Two

Introduction

John Edwards' office is on a mezzanine floor with a window overlooking the factory. While John is fetching the coffee from the vending machine, Sheila and David watch the scene below them. Work is in full swing; there are machines laid out in rows with gangways between them. There are a number of different types of machine and these are arranged in sections. On each section is a desk where the section supervisor keeps a record of the work in progress. Some workers are busy at their machines; others are moving about between sections, pushing trolleys laden with materials, parts or finished goods. At the far end is the loading bay where a fork-lift truck is loading goods on to a lorry.

Dialogue

JOHN: Here we are—three coffees. I hope I've got it right; white with no sugar, Sheila?
SHEILA: That's right, thanks very much.
JOHN: And white with sugar for you, David?
DAVID: Thanks a lot.
JOHN: Now, where were we? Oh yes, you were asking about volume of production of a new line. Well, the marketing people have some say, based on their sales forecasts. Where there's already an established market for a particular product, they try to estimate what share of that market Discovery can capture. But in the end, the Board decides how much it's prepared to invest in a product, and we're limited by that decision.
DAVID: My impression is that CP21 is something quite new.
JOHN: You're right. We've got to try to create a market for it. For this reason, if they do decide to add it to the range, it will probably be on a limited scale at first. I can't be certain, of course, but I don't see its being a big seller. I may be wrong—occasionally the most unlikely product turns out to be a winner.
SHEILA: What's a pre-production run?
JOHN: Sometimes, before we go into full production of an item, we run off a small batch—say 50 or 100—and then literally try to break them.
SHEILA: Whatever do you mean—with a hammer?
JOHN: No—simply by subjecting them to the roughest

treatment they're likely to receive in normal use. For example, a pallet for handling materials in a factory would be thrown around and dropped and have heavy items thrown on to it—just to see what it would stand up to. It's a way of identifying design weaknesses at an early stage.

DAVID: What does this reference to Health and Safety on the product sheet mean?

JOHN: The Health and Safety Act lays down requirements about safety and welfare in all places of employment. Companies—or employees—who contravene any of the rules may be liable to heavy penalties. For example, machines must be properly guarded, fire regulations observed, workers issued with the correct protective clothing, proper washing and toilet facilities provided, and so on.

DAVID: And is this your responsibility in some way?

JOHN: Only in respect of my own product. I just have to check that when it goes into production, everything about it complies with all the rules.

SHEILA: I see you've got *patent clearance* as a heading. I thought Mr Miles dealt with that?

JOHN: He takes care of the formalities, but it's normally R & D who initiate a patent application. They invent something, write the specification and discuss it with Mr Pound and Mr Blake. If it's decided to apply for a patent, they send all the papers to Mr Miles and he takes the necessary steps.

DAVID: Are patents expensive?

JOHN: A provisional patent application doesn't cost a great deal to file, and it protects the invention while our engineers are developing it. Later on, if the product looks interesting, it's submitted to the Board. If they approve, Mr Miles proceeds with the patent application. The eventual cost may be quite high—renewal fees, patent agents' fees and so on—but if it gives us the edge over the competition it's considered worth while.

SHEILA: What does *distribution* cover?

JOHN: All the processes involved in getting the goods from the factory to the eventual user—either directly or through our distributors.

DAVID: Do we have our own delivery vehicles?

JOHN: We have a small fleet for local deliveries; for long-distance trips we sometimes use private haulage contractors and sometimes the national carriers. The Despatch and Transport Manager decides which method is the most suitable.

DAVID: When will the Advertising Section become involved with CP21?

JOHN: Not until—and unless–we decide to go into production.

Then of course your people will be asked to prepare a sales leaflet, a package design and possibly some press advertising.
SHEILA: Well, it seems as though you have your hands full, John.
JOHN: Oh, yes, there's plenty to keep me busy! Now, have we covered everything you want to ask about?
DAVID: Personally, I don't think I could take any more in just at present!
SHEILA: Neither could I!
JOHN: Right then—let's go to lunch!

Lesson Notes

Work is in full swing = All the workers are fully occupied; the factory is in full operation.
The marketing people have some say = the opinion of the marketing people is taken into consideration.
a big seller, a winner = a very successful product
to stand up to (wear, rough treatment, etc.) = to resist without suffering serious damage
the eventual cost = the final cost
If it gives us the edge ... = if it gives us an advantage
to have one's hands full = to be fully occupied, very busy
to keep someone busy = to give them plenty to do; to cause them to work
to take in (information) = to absorb, understand

Grammar

The main points introduced in this Episode are:
58   The past continuous tense
59   *unless* and *until*

Drills

A

a particular product   an established market for a particular product
there's already an established market for a particular product
capture.   Discovery can capture.   what share of that market Discovery can capture.   they try to estimate what share of that market Discovery can capture.
Where there's already an established market for a particular product, they try to estimate what share of that market Discovery can capture.

quite high,   may be quite high,   the eventual cost may be quite high,
it's considered worth while.   over the competition, it's considered worth while.   if it gives us the edge over the competition, it's considered worth while.
The eventual cost may be quite high, but if it gives us the edge over the competition it's considered worth while.

B In this drill, the Product Manager is talking to the trainees. He has made some notes of the things he wants to say.

Examples
guard machines properly	Machines must be properly guarded.
observe fire regulations	Fire regulations must be observed.

provide washing facilities
install sufficient toilets
wear protective clothing
keep floors clean
provide first aid facilities
maintain adequate temperature

C

Examples
Are we going to market the product?	If we decide to market the product, it will probably be on a limited scale at first.
Are we going to start exporting?	If we decide to start exporting, it will probably be on a limited scale at first.

Are we going to recruit graduates?
Are we going to run training schemes?
Are we going to introduce incentive schemes?
Are we going to start a savings scheme?

D

Examples

What does Health and Safety cover? (fire regulations, first aid)
What does publicity cover? (advertising, press releases)

It covers such things as fire regulations, first aid and so on.
It covers such things as advertising, press releases and so on.

What does transport cover? (delivery vehicles, salesmen's cars)
What does sales promotion cover? (display material, mailing campaigns)
What does *office services* cover? (postal services, typewriter maintenance)
What does *Management Services* cover? (work study, budget forecasting)

Comprehension

1. Describe the scene from John Edwards' office window.
2. Is there an established market for CP21?
3. What does John Edwards think of the prospects for CP21?
4. What is the purpose of a pre-production run?
5. Is John Edwards in any way responsible for safety in the factory?
6. How is a patent application normally initiated?
7. Are patents expensive?
8. What does *distribution* cover?
9. Who is responsible for deliveries in the Discovery organization?
10. Is the Advertising Section involved with CP21 yet?
11. What will the Advertising Section be asked to do, if CP21 goes ahead?
12. How do David and Sheila feel at the end of their meeting with John Edwards?

19 The Sales Convention—One

Introduction

Next day, Sheila learns from June Barrett, Mr Blake's Personal Assistant, that a start is being made on the arrangements for the annual sales convention. This is a two-day event which the Marketing Department organizes every year and which is attended by all the regional managers and salesmen. The first day of the convention opens with the Chairman's review of the previous year; this is followed by a talk by the Manufacturing Director about plans for the year ahead, new products in the pipeline and any other matters directly concerned with production. The remainder of the day is devoted to training sessions designed to improve selling and marketing techniques, and also to draw the salesmen's attention to current trends in industry which may affect the demand for the company's products.

The second day consists of further training sessions, a review of overseas activities by the Overseas Director, films, short talks by departmental and section heads and opportunities for informal discussion. In the evening, the Chairman and his fellow-directors entertain the managers, the visiting salesmen and their respective wives at a cocktail party.

Dialogue

JUNE: Morning, Sheila!
SHEILA: (*Yawning*) Morning, June!
JUNE: You sound sleepy! Did you have a late night?
SHEILA: Mm. I stayed up to watch the late movie.
JUNE: Well, you'd better wake up. We've got work to do.
SHEILA: What's going on?
JUNE: The annual sales convention. We have to start on the arrangements.
SHEILA: What happens at a sales convention?
JUNE: It's partly a refresher course for the salesmen and partly an exercise in staff relations. We organize training sessions to help them keep their sales technique up to scratch, and tell them what new products are in the pipeline, what the competition is up to, and so on. There are talks by the various heads of department, and informal discussions to give the people from the different regions a chance to get to know each other and compare notes. They also have the opportunity to ask questions about any aspect of the company's activities. It

all helps to make them feel part of the company as a whole.
SHEILA: Who organizes the talks?
JUNE: Mr Green and Mr Mather arrange the details between them. Frank Davies is the Training Manager and he gives the sales lectures. His speciality is case-studies—he organizes people into syndicates. It's all very high-powered!
SHEILA: I don't understand—what are *syndicates* and *case-studies?*
JUNE: The salesmen are split into small groups, and each group is given a project or problem of some kind to work on. The groups discuss their projects, come up with proposals for solving the problems, and discuss their ideas with the whole class.
SHEILA: Are there any social activities or is it all work?
JUNE: Well, it's not what I'd call work. I think some of the reps themselves think of it as a couple of days off. And there's a cocktail party at the end of the second day.
SHEILA: Do the reps bring their wives?
JUNE: Most of them do. The company pays their hotel and travel expenses.
SHEILA: So—where do we begin?
JUNE: Here's last year's programme. Mr Blake wants us to use it as the basis for a draft for this year.

Lesson Notes

up to scratch = up to a good standard
what the competition is up to = what our competitors are doing
The question *What is . . . up to?* implies that we believe the person or organization we are speaking about is engaged in some activity which is contrary to our own interests. The phrase is often used to children. *What have you been up to?* implies that we think the child has been misbehaving in some way.
The groups . . . come up with proposals—i.e. agree/decide on/put forward proposals.
a couple of days off = two days' holiday
It's all very high-powered! = It's very stimulating, intensive, dynamic.

Drills

A

up to scratch. sales techniques up to scratch. keep their sales techniques up to scratch. to help them keep their sales techniques up to scratch.

training sessions   we organize training sessions
We organize training sessions to help them keep their sales techniques up to scratch.

in the pipeline   what new products are in the pipeline   we tell them what new products are in the pipeline
and so on.   is up to, and so on.   what the competition is up to, and so on.
We tell them what new products are in the pipeline, what the competition is up to, and so on.

discuss their projects   the groups discuss their projects
solving the problems,   proposals for solving the
problems,   come up with proposals for solving the problems,
the whole class.   with the whole class.   discuss their ideas with the whole class.
The groups discuss their projects, come up with proposals for solving the problems, and discuss their ideas with the whole class.

B

Examples

When did you join the company? (two years)	I joined the company two years ago.
When did Mr Mather join? (1970)	He joined in 1970.
How long has Mr Mather been with the Company (1970)	He's been with the company since 1970.

When did Mr Miles become Company Secretary? (1974)
When was John Edwards appointed Product Manager? (two weeks)
How long has John Edwards been Product Manager? (19th November)
When was the last Sales Convention held? (a year)
When was the first Sales Convention held? (1969)
How long has the Company been in Birmingham? (1965)

C

Examples

I'm catching the 5 o'clock train.   He said he was catching the 5 o'clock train.

Type the letters this afternoon.   He told me to type the letters this afternoon.

Get Mr Green on the phone.
I'm going over to the factory.
I'll be back in time to sign the letters.
Order a taxi for me, please.
Find out what time my train arrives.
I shan't be in the office to-morrow.
Give me a ring if there's anything important.
Send the letters first class.

Comprehension

1 Why is Sheila so tired this morning?
2 Who is June Barrett?
3 What job are the two girls about to start on?
4 Who is chiefly responsible for organizing the sales convention?
5 What does a sales convention consist of?
6 What does the company hope to achieve by holding this event?
7 How often does Discovery Engineering hold a sales convention?
8 What training methods are used?
9 What are the objectives of the training sessions?
10 What social activities take place?
11 How do some of the salesmen regard the event?
12 Do the salesmen's wives attend the convention?
13 What is a *case study?*
14 How do the girls set about drafting the programme?

20 The Sales Convention—Two

Introduction

June and Sheila spend much of the morning compiling a draft programme for the forthcoming sales convention. As well as last year's programme, June produces a file containing all the correspondence and memoranda referring to the convention arrangements—details of hotel reservations, catering arrangements, the hire of reception and conference rooms and so forth. It is normal for the head of each department and section to be available at some time during the informal periods so that the salesmen can raise queries or make suggestions to improve efficiency.

The Advertising Section mounts a small exhibition, which generally includes photographs showing the company's products in use in customers' premises, details of projects of special interest (both at home and overseas) and information about any new products. This year, the new product BI99 is to be launched during the convention.

Dialogue

SHEILA: I can see why we have to start planning the convention well in advance!

JUNE: Yes, there's a lot of work involved. But it's interesting, and the convention itself is quite good fun.

SHEILA: Where's it held?

JUNE: At the Castle Hotel. They have conference facilities, and most of the salesmen and their wives stay there. We pretty well take the place over for a couple of days.

SHEILA: Do the salesmen call in at the offices while they're here?

JUNE: Some of them drop in for a chat. It's nice to meet them in the flesh, after talking to them on the phone during the year.

SHEILA: How do the wives spend their time while their husbands are at the convention?

JUNE: Oh, they go into town shopping, or to the cinema or exhibitions—there's always plenty to do in Birmingham. Last year we organized a tour of the works and offices for them; that went down very well.

SHEILA: I don't suppose they'll want to see it all again this year?

JUNE: Well, some of them will be here for the first time.

SHEILA: You mean the ones whose husbands joined the company during the year?
JUNE: That's right—or the ones who got married during the year. There are usually quite a few new faces every year.
SHEILA: Have we finished the draft?
JUNE: I don't think we can go any further with the details until Mr Blake has had a look at it. What we can do now is to make a start on the correspondence. I've already booked the Castle on the phone, but we must write a letter of confirmation. Then we have to write memos to all the regional managers, giving them the dates and asking them to let us know how many of their people will be bringing their wives, and so on. And the managers here at head office must all be reminded of the dates, to make sure they're around to give their little talks.
SHEILA: By the way, I see there's a new product being introduced. That's not CP21, surely?
JUNE: Oh no—it'll be months before that one gets off the ground. This is BI99.
SHEILA: Of course—the one David Long's been doing the brochure for. I wonder how he's getting on with it.
JUNE: Well, you can go and ask him this afternoon. When all the memos are ready, perhaps you'd like to go round and deliver them. It'll give you a chance to find your way around some of the other offices.
SHEILA: All right. Is there anything else you'd like me to do?
JUNE: Give me a hand with the typing, will you?
SHEILA: Sure. Is it all right if I use this machine?
JUNE: Yes, of course. I think you'll find everything you need in the top drawer of that desk.

•
Lesson Notes

quite good fun = enjoyable, entertaining, amusing
pretty well = almost entirely (compare with *more or less*)
That went down very well = everyone enjoyed it
to drop in = to pay an informal visit
in the flesh = in person
around = present, available
to get off the ground = to make a satisfactory beginning.
Give me a hand with the typing, will you? This should not be confused with the question tag. It is merely a variation of the polite request *Will you give me a hand with the typing, please?*, but it is an informal style of speaking which one would use to a colleague or subordinate, but not normally to a superior.

Grammar

The main points introduced in this Episode are:
60 *to be* plus infinitive
61 *until* followed by present perfect tense

Drills

A

well in advance!   planning the convention well in advance!   to start planning the convention well in advance!   why we have to start planning the convention well in advance!
I can see why we have to start planning the convention well in advance!

letter of confirmation.   we must write a letter of confirmation.   on the phone,   booked the Castle on the phone,   I've already booked the Castle on the phone,
I've already booked the Castle on the phone, but we must write a letter of confirmation.

the other offices.   around some of the other offices.   find your way around some of the other offices.   a chance to find your way around some of the other offices.
It'll give you a chance to find your way around some of the other offices.

like me to do?   anything else you'd like me to do?
Is there anything else you'd like me to do?

B

Examples

What happens at a sales convention? (training sessions/lectures)	There are training sessions and lectures.
What's happening to-day? (Frank Davies/give/lecture)	Frank Davies is giving a lecture.
What happens in a training session? (syndicates and case-studies)	There are syndicates and case-studies.
What's happening to-day? (Frank/organize/case-study)	Frank's organizing a case-study.

What happens at a Board Meeting? (Directors/discuss/company business)

What's happening at to-day's meeting? (Directors/discuss/CP21)
Who runs the Advertising Section? (Mrs Wood)
Who's preparing the B199 leaflet? (David Long)
Who organizes the sales convention? (Marketing Department)
Who's helping June this year? (Sheila Smith)
What happens at a product evaluation meeting? (Product committee/consider/new products)
What's happening at to-day's meeting? (Committee/consider/CP21)

C

Examples

Do the salesmen bring their wives?	Some of them do.
Are the salesmen married?	Some of them are.

Do the salesmen stay at the Castle Hotel?
Have they got company cars?
Do they come to the convention by car?
Are the management trainees women?
Have the trainees got degrees?
Are the products exported?
Do the products sell well abroad?

Comprehension

1. How do June and Sheila spend much of the morning?
2. What kind of arrangements are necessary when planning the sales convention?
3. Where is the convention held?
4. Why is it necessary to start planning the convention well in advance?
5. How does June feel about the convention?

6 How do the salesmen's wives amuse themselves during the day?
7 Does the company organize anything for them?
8 Why are there new faces every year?
9 What matters must be dealt with by correspondence?
10 Why must managers be reminded of the convention dates?
11 Which new product is being launched at the convention?
12 Why does June suggest that Sheila delivers the memos?

21 A Tour of the Offices

Introduction

June and Sheila spend the rest of the morning typing the letters and internal memoranda about the sales convention. When they have finished, June takes all the correspondence to Mr Blake for signature. She also shows him the draft programme for the convention that she and Sheila have prepared. Mr Blake adds *Overseas Review* to the list of items, explaining that he has asked for this so that the UK salesmen can learn something of the company's activities abroad. Otherwise he approves the draft and hands it back to June.

June mentions that she has asked Sheila to deliver the internal memoranda in order that she may learn the layout of the building. Mr Blake thinks it will be better if June goes with her, to show her where the various departments are located.

Dialogue

JUNE: Here we are, Sheila—Mr Blake has signed all the letters and memos.
SHEILA: I hope he didn't find any typing errors in the ones I did!
JUNE: Don't worry, they were all OK. Now, I told Mr Blake I'd suggested that you go round with them, and he said I should come with you and introduce you to everyone.
SHEILA: That's a relief! I was scared I'd get lost if I went by myself.
JUNE: You'll soon find your way around. Now, we'll go to the post room first with the letters.
SHEILA: I thought they were collected by the messenger.
JUNE: So they are, but you might as well know where the post room is in case you ever have any queries. Besides, the stationery stores and copying section are all in the same room ... here we are. Good morning, Mr Perkins. I've brought a newcomer to meet you. Mr Perkins—Miss Smith.
SHEILA: How do you do, Mr Perkins.
PERKINS: How do you do, Miss Smith. Just started, have you?
SHEILA: This is my third week, actually. I'm gradually finding out where everyone lives.
JUNE: Mr Perkins is in charge of office services: internal and external post, stationery stores, duplicating, typewriter maintenance, office cleaning, all that sort of thing. I don't know what we'd do without him!

PERKINS: What can we do for you to-day, Miss Barrett?
JUNE: Well, I'm just showing Miss Smith round the building, but perhaps we could leave these letters while we're here. Have you anything for us, by the way?
PERKINS: Yes, there are some letters for Mr Blake. Here you are.
JUNE: Many thanks. Cheerio ... Now, where have we to go next? Ah yes, we'll go over to the works and I'll show you where Mr Pound's office is.
SHEILA: He's the Manufacturing Director, isn't he?
JUNE: Right. I don't suppose for a moment that he'll be in his office—he's usually missing when anyone wants him. The girls on the switchboard are always having to put out calls for him.
SHEILA: Where's the switchboard?
JUNE: It's on the ground floor—behind the reception desk. I'll show you on the way back. After that we'll go to the Chairman's office, then to the Overseas Department, and finally the Secretarial and Accounts Departments. It should be lunch-time by then!

Lesson Notes

I was scared I'd get lost = I was afraid I should get lost.
I thought they were collected by the messenger. So they are ...
Do not confuse *so they are*, which confirms the first statement, with *so are they*.
might as well (invariable) + infinitive. This is an idiomatic construction which conveys a mild feeling of obligation, necessity or inevitability.
You might as well know where the post room is i.e. because this information will be useful.
We might as well go home—because there is no reason to remain.
Just started, have you? = an informal variation of the simple question *Have you just started?*
besides = in addition
actually = in fact
I don't suppose for a moment ... = I think it very unlikely
missing = absent
to put out a call = to relay a message on a public loudspeaker system
It should be lunch-time by then = it will probably/almost certainly be lunch-time.

Grammar

The main point introduced in this Episode is:
62 Omission of *that* before an object clause

Comprehension

1. How do June and Sheila spend the rest of the morning?
2. What does June do with the correspondence?
3. What else does she show Mr Blake?
4. What addition does he make to the draft programme?
5. Why does he want this additional item?
6. What does June tell Mr Blake that she has suggested to Sheila?
7. What is his reaction?
8. Why is Sheila relieved to hear what Mr Blake has suggested?
9. What is Mr Perkins responsible for?
10. What does he give to June?
11. What problems does Mr Pound cause for the girls on the switchboard?
12. When does June expect to finish delivering all the correspondence?

22 Training Opportunities

Introduction

Sheila and David are having lunch together in the canteen. They find Mr Green's secretary, Ruth Taylor, sitting alone at a table by the window and she invites them to sit with her. Over lunch, the trainees discuss their impressions of Discovery Engineering so far. Ruth has been working for the company for five years; she joined straight from school as a junior in the accounts department. She studied shorthand and typewriting at evening classes for which the company paid, and was promoted to her present job after two years. She tells Sheila and David about some of the training schemes run by the company and mentions that she is now considering taking a further course of study.

Dialogue

SHEILA: Hullo, Ruth. Are you keeping these seats for someone?

RUTH: No, please join me. I usually have lunch with some friends, but I'm later than usual to-day. I had to send an urgent telex.

DAVID: How long have you been here, Ruth?

RUTH: Just over five years. I became Mr Green's secretary nearly three years ago.

SHEILA: And we've been with Discovery for exactly a month to-day!

RUTH: How are you getting on?

SHEILA: Not too badly—how about you, David?

DAVID: Oh, I'm enjoying myself very much. We're going to be very busy for the next few weeks, though.

SHEILA: Making your exhibit for the sales convention?

RUTH: It's always hectic around convention time. I'm up to my eyes in arrangements for the training sessions.

SHEILA: It must cost the company a great deal of money. Is it worth it, do you think?

RUTH: Yes, I do. Apart from the training aspect, I think it makes for better communications between the management and the people in the regions.

DAVID: The management seem pretty approachable.

RUTH: Yes, they are. Anyone can have an interview with a director or head of department if they've got something on their mind. And suggestions and bright ideas are welcomed from anyone.

SHEILA: Has there ever been a strike at Discovery?

RUTH: Not to my knowledge. The management pride themselves on maintaining good industrial relations. There's a works meeting every month between Mr Pound and the various section heads and supervisors in the Production Department. Mr Pound has a great reputation as a trouble-shooter.

SHEILA: What's a *trouble-shooter?*

DAVID: Someone who spots a potential source of trouble and nips it in the bud before it becomes serious or gets out of hand.

SHEILA: I see.

DAVID: Are there any training schemes for the factory workers?

RUTH: There are two schemes in operation at present—one for craft apprentices and one for technicians. On top of that the company will help anyone who wants to follow an outside course.

SHEILA: Do you mean at evening classes?

RUTH: Yes, or on a day-release basis, or sometimes even a correspondence course.

SHEILA: How about the Open University?

RUTH: I don't actually know of anyone doing an Open University course, but I dare say the management would be sympathetic if they were approached about it. I think the person would have to satisfy them that the course was relevant to his or her job, though.

DAVID: How does a day release course operate?

RUTH: You apply for permission to attend college on one complete day a week. Your manager has to approve the course. I'm thinking of doing the HNC in Business Studies.

SHEILA: What does HNC stand for?

RUTH: Higher National Certificate.

DAVID: And will the company pay your fees?

RUTH: That's what I'm hoping. They sometimes pay for textbooks as well, or give you a grant or loan towards the cost of them.

DAVID: However will Mr Green manage without you if you're away one whole day a week?

RUTH: One of the girls in the typing pool will do any urgent letters for him on the days when I'm at college.

SHEILA: You'll just have to work twice as hard on the other days!

RUTH: I guess so!

SHEILA: Well, I'll have to leave you, I'm afraid. I've got some shopping to do. See you later.

RUTH: Me too—I'll come with you. So long, David.

DAVID: 'Bye, girls!

Lesson Notes

She joined straight from school = she came to work for the company immediately after leaving school.
I think it makes for better communication ... = I think it leads to/helps to bring about better communication.
I'm up to my eyes in ... *(coll.)* = I'm fully occupied, very busy.
Anyone can have an interview ... *if they've got something on their mind.* Since *anyone* may refer to either a man or a woman, we must either say *if he or she* ... *on his or her mind*, which is clumsy, or use the impersonal *they* and *their* which is normally preferred in conversation.
The management seem pretty approachable. Yes, they are. This habit of treating a singular subject as if it were plural is normal when the subject is a collective noun indicating a group of people. However, *The management seems pretty approachable* is also correct and the distinction lies chiefly in the speaker's mind, and whether he is considering *management* as a corporate body or as a group of individual members. *Government* is another word which is frequently used in the same way.
to pride oneself (on something) = to be proud of. The expression is used chiefly when speaking of an achievement or a state of affairs.
to spot = to notice, observe
to nip (a potential problem) in the bud = to solve it before it becomes serious
out of hand = out of control
on top of = in addition to
I dare say = I think it probable or possible.
Me too! This is a colloquial, informal way of saying *So have I, So do I, So am I* etc.

Comprehension

1. How long has Ruth been working for Discovery Engineering?
2. How long have David and Sheila been with the company?
3. How did Ruth reach her present position as secretary to Mr Green?
4. Why is Ruth lunching on her own to-day?
5. Is Ruth particularly busy at present?
6. What is her opinion of the sales convention?
7. Describe the attitude of the management of Discovery Engineering towards its employees' problems.
8. How good is the company's industrial relations record?
9. How does it maintain good industrial relations?

10 What training schemes does Discovery offer its employees?
11 What course is Ruth thinking of following?
12 How will Mr Green manage on the days when she is at college?

23 More Preparations for the Convention

Introduction

David and Mrs Wood are discussing the display which the Advertising Section is going to mount for the sales convention. A small exhibition unit has been constructed to take samples of the company's products. The unit incorporates a show-case; a selection of photographs will be arranged on display panels at the back of the unit. The focal point of the arrangement is to be BI99, the new product which will be launched at the convention. It is also the product for which David drafted a brochure during his first week at Discovery.

While they are planning the display, David mentions that he is a linguist, and Mrs Wood thinks that he might be called upon to act as an interpreter for the company during an international trade fair to be held in Birmingham later in the year.

Dialogue

MRS WOOD: We're going to have our work cut out to get all these items in the show-case. I should have asked for a larger one.

DAVID: Is it possible to increase the size of the unit?

MRS WOOD: I'm afraid not—there isn't time. We shall just have to manage.

DAVID: How do you want the stuff arranged?

MRS WOOD: Well of course BI99 is the thing they'll all want to look at. We'll have to allocate plenty of space for that. By the way, has your brochure been finally approved?

DAVID: Yes, I had the draft back from Mr Blake this morning. There's a note awaiting your signature, giving the printers their instructions.

MRS WOOD: Well done! You did a good job there.

DAVID: Thanks very much. We're surely not going to market the product as BI99, I suppose?

MRS WOOD: No, of course not. In fact, there's a meeting going on at the moment to make the final choice of name—there have been one or two quite good suggestions. We'll have to add the name to your draft once we know what it's going to be.

DAVID: Yes, all right. About this unit—how about mounting the smaller items on display panels and leaving the show-case for the heavier ones?

MRS WOOD: Good idea. We've got some heavy-duty panels here as well as light-weight ones for photographs.
DAVID: There are dozens of photos in this folder—are we going to use them all?
MRS WOOD: No, only a selection. Let's spread them out and have a look at them.
DAVID: Has our own photographer taken all these?
MRS WOOD: All except the overseas ones.
DAVID: Do we do much overseas business?
MRS WOOD: We did very little up till about five years ago. Then we took part in an international trade fair and took several thousand pounds' worth of export orders in a couple of days. Since then our export trade has built up steadily.
DAVID: There's a trade fair coming up later this year, isn't there?
MRS WOOD: Yes, in October. It's being held at the new exhibition centre here in Birmingham. That's our next important job once this convention is out of the way.
DAVID: Where are our principal overseas markets?
MRS WOOD: Chiefly in Europe and the States, but we have begun to reach the Middle East, South America and Australasia.
DAVID: Do many of the foreign buyers speak English?
MRS WOOD: A lot of them do, but not all. Our directors are beginning to realize that our overseas people ought to be able to speak some foreign languages. Of course, there are interpreting and translating services at the exhibition centre—we can't hope to cover every possible language.
DAVID: Perhaps I could be of some use as an interpreter. I did my degree in modern languages.
MRS WOOD: Did you? That's interesting.
DAVID: Actually, I was told at my interview that the company was hoping to extend its overseas activities. I made a mental note at the time to try and find out more about it.
MRS WOOD: Have you spent much time overseas?
DAVID: I spent several vacations abroad while I was at University.
MRS WOOD: Well, we must bear all this in mind when we get down to detailed plans for the exhibition. Meanwhile, we'd better get on with this one! Pass me those photos, will you please?

Lesson Notes

We're going to have our work cut out to get all these items in the show-case = It is going to be difficult to get ...

stuff (coll.) = things, material, items, possessions etc.
We shall just have to manage = We shall have to do the job with the materials we already have.
I had the draft back . . . this morning = I received the draft back/the draft was returned to me this morning.
There's a trade fair coming up. coming up indicates that an event or time is approaching. *What's the time? It's coming up to* (= it's nearly) *two o'clock.*
out of the way = over, completed, dealt with
I did my degree in languages. Did you? That's interesting. The short question response is not intended to express doubt; it merely acknowledges the information given. It is often followed, as in this case, by a further comment or a question.
I spoke to Mr Blake this morning. Did you? What did he say?
I can't find my briefcase. Can't you? Perhaps it's in your car.

Grammar

The main point introduced in this Episode is:
63   ought

Comprehension

1. What are Mrs Wood and David doing in this Episode?
2. Are they finding the job easy?
3. What is the problem?
4. What is the principal exhibit of the display?
5. What name is BI99 going to be marketed under?
6. What suggestion does David make for mounting the items for the display?
7. Did the company's own photographer take all the photographs?
8. Does the company do much overseas business?
9. What happened at the trade fair five years ago?
10. What is the next important job for the Advertising Section?
11. Where are Discovery Engineering's principal export markets?
12. Why is David particularly interested in the company's overseas activities?
13. What new policy is the company following with regard to overseas activities?
14. Did Mrs Wood already know that David was a linguist?

24 At the Castle Hotel

Introduction

Everyone connected with the sales convention has been working very hard for several weeks. To-day is the eve of the convention, and final preparations are being made. At the Castle Hotel, the conference suite has been laid out under the combined supervision of Mr Green and Mr Blake to accommodate the programme of lectures, films and case-studies that has been prepared. One room has been converted into a temporary cinema for the screening of films; the windows have been blacked out and a projector installed. Mrs Wood and David Long have been arranging their display on the stand which has been erected in the vestibule by two employees from the company's maintenance section.

June Barrett is responsible for liaison with the hotel management, and Sheila has been helping her. After ensuring that all the arrangements for the conference programme are going smoothly, they go across to the main part of the hotel to make a final check on the accommodation and catering arrangements. While they are talking to the receptionist, a man comes into the hotel and walks over to the reception desk.

Dialogue

RECEPTIONIST: Good afternoon, sir. Can I help you?
MORGAN: Good afternoon. Have you a single room with bathroom for to-night, please?
RECEPTIONIST: I'm very sorry, sir. All I have left is a single room with shower.
MORGAN: That'll do. Which floor is it on?
RECEPTIONIST: It's on the third floor, at the back of the hotel. No. 321. What name is it please, sir?
MORGAN: Morgan. Owen Morgan.
RECEPTIONIST: How long will you be staying, Mr Morgan?
MORGAN: Just one night.
RECEPTIONIST: Will you fill in this form, please?
MORGAN: Yes, of course. (Under his breath) Name, nationality Welsh, address, company address, car registration number. Here you are.
RECEPTIONIST: Thank you. Would you like early morning tea?
MORGAN: Yes, please—at eight o'clock. What time do you serve meals?

RECEPTIONIST: Dinner is served from 7 o'clock until 10. Breakfast is from 7.45 until 9.15. Would you like to order a morning paper?
MORGAN: Yes please—the *Financial Times*.
RECEPTIONIST: Very good, sir. Here's your key. The porter will show you to your room.
MORGAN: Thanks. How do I get to the garage, please?
RECEPTIONIST: It's behind the hotel—but I'm afraid every space is reserved to-night. There's a public car park about fifty metres down the road—there's usually plenty of space there.
MORGAN: You seem to be pretty busy!
RECEPTIONIST: Yes, we are. A local company is holding its annual sales convention here.
MORGAN: I see. I suppose I'm lucky to get a room. Where did you say the car park is?
RECEPTIONIST: The entrance is on the right, just before you reach the traffic lights. It's sign-posted quite clearly—you can't miss it.
MORGAN: Thank you. Oh, there's one other thing; where's the nearest chemist?
RECEPTIONIST: There's one directly opposite the hotel, but I'm afraid it's shut. To-day is early-closing day. Perhaps we can help you—we keep supplies of toilet items, aspirins, and that sort of thing.
MORGAN: I need a packet of razor blades and some aspirins, if you have them.
RECEPTIONIST: Certainly, sir. Here you are. Shall I add them to your bill?
MORGAN: Yes, that'll be fine, thank you. Now I'd better park the car before going up to my room. I'll leave my things here if I may.
RECEPTIONIST: Of course sir, that'll be quite all right.

Lesson Notes

That'll do = that will do = that will serve the purpose/be suitable/sufficient.
going smoothly = proceeding according to plan, without problems
early-closing day. Many shops in England close for one afternoon a week, normally either Wednesday or Thursday. The day varies from one district to another but the shops in any one district close on the same afternoon.
I'll leave my things here = I'll leave my luggage here.

Comprehension

1 Who has supervised the arrangement of the conference suite for the Discovery Sales Convention?
2 What special arrangements have been made?
3 What have David and Mrs Wood been doing?
4 What is June Barrett responsible for?
5 What happens while June and Sheila are talking to the receptionist?
6 What does Mr Morgan want?
7 Can the receptionist give him exactly what he wants? Why not?
8 What alternative does she offer him?
9 Where is the hotel car park? Is it likely to be full?
10 Why is there no room for Mr Morgan's car in the hotel car park?
11 Where is the public car park?
12 Why is the chemist's shop closed?
13 How is Mr Morgan charged for his razor blades and aspirins?
14 Does Mr Morgan go straight up to his room? Why not?

25 After the Convention

Introduction

As a result of careful organization and planning, the sales convention was a great success and everyone concerned felt well satisfied with the results. The Chairman's review was particularly well received; he announced that despite difficult conditions the company was having a successful year in the home market, whilst prospects abroad had never looked brighter. The Overseas Director also spoke about plans for expansion of the company's foreign activities, which included both exporting and the setting-up of manufacturing or selling organizations in selected territories. As one or two products were coming to the end of their life cycle, the company expected to have some spare production capacity within the next few months, and the possibility of negotiating manufacturing licences with foreign concerns was being actively considered.

The convention ended with a cocktail party. Those who lived within a reasonable distance of Birmingham returned home that evening, but most of the people from the regional offices stayed at the hotel for one more night and set off for home the following morning. At the party, June Barrett was congratulated on the success of the occasion by several people, including the managers of the Scottish Regional office, Donald Baird, and of the Bristol office, Mike Allen.

Dialogue

BAIRD: Well, June—congratulations! Everything went like clockwork.
JUNE: Thanks, Donald. I'm glad you think so.
BAIRD: Let me get you another drink—your glass is empty.
JUNE: Thanks. A gin and tonic, please. I feel I've earned it!
BAIRD: You certainly have ... here you are—one gin and tonic. Cheers!
JUNE: Cheers! Oh look, here's Mike Allen. How are you, Mike?
ALLEN: Lovely to see you again, June. Full marks for the organization—as usual! You must be glad it's over.
JUNE: I can't say I'm sorry.
ALLEN: Neither can I! Those case studies of Frank's were real teasers—I shall be dreaming about them to-night!
BAIRD: I haven't seen your wife yet, Mike. Is she here?

ALLEN: She's around somewhere. I haven't seen much of her myself for the past couple of days.
JUNE: I suppose you're still a happy bachelor, Donald?
BAIRD: Bachelor—yes; happy?—maybe. I don't think any woman would be prepared to put up with me. I never seem to get home much before eight, and then I often take stuff home with me.
ALLEN: That's no good. Are you short-staffed?
BAIRD: Yes, we are really. I could do with a PA—my secretary's too young to take much responsibility. She's a good girl but there's a limit to what I can give her.
ALLEN: Yes, I know what you mean. Can't you recruit a more senior person?
BAIRD: I've been trying to get old Blake to agree to it but I'm having a job to convince him it's necessary. I'll swear he thinks it's just bad organization on my part. Anyway, how are things in the South-West?
ALLEN: Oh, mustn't grumble! We exceeded all our targets last quarter by nearly 5% so we're feeling quite pleased with ourselves.
BAIRD: So I heard. Congratulations! And now you're going to smash all records with this new wonder product, I suppose!
ALLEN: I have my doubts about that. Between you and me, I think the Board has backed a loser there. I told Blake as much six months ago.
BAIRD: I'm surprised to hear you say that—I think it'll go well in our region. But I can see that it may not be such a hit in your part of the country.
JUNE: Look here, if you two are going to talk shop, I'm off!
ALLEN: Sorry, love! You stay here and talk to Donald. I must go and find the wife.

Lesson Notes

to set off (on a journey) = to leave, to depart
over = finished, ended
I haven't seen much of her . . . = I have spent very little time with her.
to put up with = to tolerate, endure
I often take stuff home with me. Stuff literally means a substance, or the material from which something is made, but it is used in a number of idiomatic expressions with slightly different meanings. Here it means work (e.g. letters, files, reports etc.) which the speaker takes home because he has no time to deal with it during normal office hours. The words *with me* give a slight extra

emphasis but do not otherwise affect the meaning of the phrase. *Those case studies of Frank's were real teasers.* This is an example of the *double genitive* which is explained fully in the grammar section.
to get home=to reach home
short-staffed=in need of additional staff
PA=personal assistant
I'm having a job to convince him . . . *(coll.)*=I'm finding it difficult to convince him.
I'll swear he thinks . . . *(coll.)*= I'm sure he thinks
I think the Board has backed a loser (coll.)= I think the Board has decided to invest in a product which will not prove successful. Compare with *a winner* in Episode 18.
I told Blake as much=I told him the same thing.
a hit=a success
to talk shop=to talk about business on a social occasion
I'm off!(coll.)=I'm leaving.
I must go and find the wife. This is a colloquial variation of . . . find (or look for) *my* wife.

Grammar

The main point introduced in this Episode is:
64 The double genitive

Drills

A

Examples

I'm studying for my HNC. What did she say?	She said she was studying for her HNC.
I'm learning shorthand and typing. What did she say?	She said she was learning shorthand and typing.

I'm going to evening classes.
What did she say?
I want to get promotion.
What did she say?
I'll have to study very hard.
What did she say?
But I think it'll be worth it.
What did she say?

B

Examples

David, Sheila is typing the memos.
What did you tell David?

I told him Sheila was typing the memos.

David, they've appointed John Edwards to be Product Manager.
What did you tell David?

I told him they'd appointed John Edwards to be Product Manager.

David, we're having lunch in the canteen.
What did you tell David?
David, Ruth is meeting us there.
What did you tell David?
David, we want to go to lunch early.
What did you tell David?
David, Mrs Wood is looking for you.
What did you tell David?

C

Examples

The sales convention costs a lot of money.
Is it worth it? (improve/staff relations).

Yes, if it improves staff relations, it's well worth it.

Ruth is studying very hard.
Is it worth it? (get better job).

Yes, if she gets a better job, it's well worth it.

The company spends a lot on advertising.
Is it worth it? (increase/sales)
We do a lot of market research.
Is it worth it? (provide/market information)
The Company runs a lot of incentive schemes.
Is it worth it? (improve/production)
The canteen is heavily subsidized.
Is it worth it? (keep/staff happy)

D

Examples

This unit is too small. (ask/large)
You should have asked for a larger one.

This house is too large. (buy/small)
You should have bought a smaller one.

This car is too expensive to run. (buy/economical)
This coat is too heavy. (wear/light)
These shoes are too thin. (wear/thick)
These chairs are uncomfortable. (buy/comfortable)

E

Examples

David did his degree in modern languages. (interesting)
Did he? That's interesting!

Our sales figures this month are a record. (congratulations)
Are they? Congratulations!

We've exceeded our targets by 5%. (well done)
Ruth has passed her exams. (that's good)
They're going to redecorate the canteen. (about time too)
The telephone is out of order. (a nuisance)

F

Examples

I missed the train. (leave/early/catch)
If you had left earlier, you would have caught it.

I lost my watch. (search/careful/find)
If you had searched more carefully, you would have found it.

I missed the bus. (walk/quick/catch)
I failed my exams. (study/hard/pass)

I missed the post. (run/fast/catch)
I missed the weather forecast. (listen/close/hear)

Comprehension

1 How did the sales convention go?
2 What did the Chairman say in his review?
3 What did the Overseas Director say about overseas activities?
4 How did the convention end?
5 Did everyone go home immediately after the convention?
6 Why did several people congratulate June?
7 Why does Donald Baird have to take work home with him?
8 Can't his secretary help?
9 Why doesn't he recruit a more senior person?
10 Why are the staff of the South-West region feeling pleased with themselves?
11 What is Mike Allen's opinion of the new product?
12 Does Donald Baird agree with him?
13 What is June's reaction to the conversation between the two men?
14 Where does Mike Allen go?

26 The Trade Fair—One

Introduction

Once the sales convention was over, all the departments concerned turned their attention to the trade fair which was to take place in the autumn. Overall responsibility for the arrangements was shared between Mr Blake, the Sales and Marketing Director, and Mr Young, the Overseas Director, but nearly every department in the company was involved in some way or other.

It was the responsibility of the Production Department to produce a complete range of the company's products with an *exhibition finish*—that is, absolutely flawless. They also had to be sure that information on delivery times for all the different lines was accurate and up to date. The Advertising Section had to see that the literature was correct and that there were adequate supplies of all the current brochures.

The manning of the stand was especially important. Buyers from many large companies, both British and overseas, would be at the exhibition and it was essential to create a good impression. In view of its increasing overseas trade, Discovery had recently made a point of recruiting staff who could speak at least one foreign language. David Long, who had a degree in modern languages, was invited to attend the meetings at which the exhibition arrangements were to be discussed. Before the first meeting, Mrs Wood gave him some background information.

Dialogue

DAVID: Where is this exhibition being held?
MRS WOOD: At the National Exhibition Centre, here in Birmingham.
DAVID: That's very handy from our point of view, isn't it?
MRS WOOD: It certainly is—it saves us a lot of time and expense in travelling and transporting our exhibits.
DAVID: Have we booked our site at the Centre?
MRS WOOD: Yes, we did that some weeks ago. We've just received the floor plan. Here it is; we've been given stand No. 50 in Hall No. 3.
DAVID: Don't we get a choice?
MRS WOOD: Well, when we filled in our application form, we specified our requirements—size, services required, type of product to be exhibited and so on. All the other exhibitors do

the same, and stands are allocated accordingly. If the one allocated to us doesn't suit us, then naturally we take it up with the exhibition organizers.

DAVID: Who are they?

MRS WOOD: An independent, specialist company which arranges exhibitions for trade and manufacturers' associations. They take complete charge of the organization and administration of the exhibition, including things like publicity and information services, customs clearance for overseas exhibitors and so on.

DAVID: Why customs clearance?

MRS WOOD: Special arrangements exist so that goods for exhibition purposes may be imported duty free. Customs officials are in attendance while the exhibits are being brought in.

DAVID: Do the organizers build the stands?

MRS WOOD: At some exhibitions, they provide basic *shells* or *modules* which the exhibitors then complete themselves. In others, the exhibitors design and build their own stands from scratch—as we're doing in this case.

DAVID: Do we actually construct the stands ourselves?

MRS WOOD: No, we employ a firm of contractors who specialize in this kind of work. One of their people will be at to-day's meeting to discuss the design of our stand.

DAVID: Presumably we give them some guidance on the sort of thing we want?

MRS WOOD: Of course. We draw up a list of criteria—range of products to be displayed, amenities to be provided, how many staff we expect to have on duty at any one time, and so on. They come back with an estimate of the amount of space we shall need. Once this is agreed we book our space through the organizers. Then the contractor gets down to the job of producing a detailed design for the stand. That's what to-day's meeting is about.

DAVID: What sort of amenities are we thinking of?

MRS WOOD: Well, if we have an important visitor who looks like a potential customer—or if one of our *regulars* comes to visit us—we can't keep him standing about indefinitely. We must have an area where we can sit and talk to our visitors and where they can study our brochures if they wish. We also have to include a small office for June with a phone and somewhere to keep publicity material, and so on.

DAVID: I can see it's quite a major undertaking.

MRS WOOD: You're right; in effect, we have to set up a miniature sales department for the period of the exhibition. People who visit these events don't always realize what a lot of work goes on behind the scenes.

Lesson Notes

trade fair=trade exhibition. The terms are interchangeable.
manning=operating
to make a point of (followed by the -*ing* form of a verb)=to pay special attention to, attach special importance to
from scratch=from the very beginning, from zero
amenities=services and facilities such as a telephone, electricity, water etc.
They come back with an estimate . . . =They prepare an estimate, based on the information we have given them, and send it to us. Compare this idiom (to come back with) with *to come up with* in Episode 19.
to take a matter up with someone=to speak to that person about it
regulars=regular customers
to set up=to establish
The Advertising Section had to see that the literature was correct=The Section had to make sure that . . .
to see to (something)=to take care of, to be responsible for

Comprehension

1 Who is chiefly responsible for the arrangements for the trade fair?
2 What other departments are involved?
3 What are the Production Department's main responsibilities?
4 What must the Advertising Section see to?
5 What particular qualification has Discovery Engineering been seeking lately, when recruiting staff?
6 What is David's qualification?
7 Where is the trade exhibition being held?
8 How does one set about booking space at a trade exhibition?
9 Why is it necessary for customs officials to attend at the exhibition hall?
10 Do the organizers provide the stands?
11 What amenities are needed on the Discovery stand?
12 How is a stand designed?
13 How can the choice of staff to man the stand affect the impression given to customers?
14 What are the advantages to Discovery Engineering of exhibiting at the National Exhibition Centre?
15 What is the function of an exhibition organiser?

27 The Trade Fair—Two

Introduction

David Long attended the first meeting at which detailed arrangements for the forthcoming trade fair were discussed. He had been asked to do so because, as a linguist, he was to be included in the team to man the company's stand and act as an interpreter if required. Mr Young, the Overseas Director, who also spoke several foreign languages, briefed him on his duties after a further meeting, called a few days before the fair was due to open to finalize the arrangements.

Construction of the stand was well up to schedule. There had been some hitches in the production of certain exhibits, due to a series of minor breakdowns in the factory, but these problems had been overcome and everything was expected to be ready on time. The exhibition organizers had supplied various exhibition aids, such as visitor invitations, information leaflets, stickers and posters, which the company had been using to publicize its stand. It was hoped to attract many foreign buyers to the Discovery exhibit as the company was particularly anxious to boost sales abroad.

Dialogue

YOUNG: Now, David, you and I between us have got to supply the interpreting services on the Discovery stand. Do you think you can manage?

DAVID: I'll do my best. I've studied all our brochures and I feel pretty confident that I can interpret those. Of course, people may ask questions that aren't answered in our literature.

YOUNG: Don't worry—you won't be left on your own. Either Mr Blake or myself, or one of our deputies, will be on duty throughout the exhibition and there'll normally be a production engineer around to help with technical queries. June Barrett will be there as well, to look after the admin. I think your friend Sheila Smith will be helping her.

DAVID: What exactly do you want me to do?

YOUNG: Your main job will be to help the staff on the stand with any language problems that may arise, but you may be called upon to handle some routine enquiries yourself if we get really busy.

DAVID: I hope I shall be able to cope. I've only been with the company for a short time, you know.

YOUNG: That's all right. If you're in any doubt, just keep the customer happy until one of us is free to come to the rescue. A lot of people just want to stop long enough to pick up a few catalogues. Try to get their names, and the names and addresses of their companies, so that we can follow up the enquiries after the exhibition.

DAVID: What arrangements are there for meals?

YOUNG: Oh, there are several restaurants and bars. We'll arrange a rota so that there's always someone on duty on the stand, even during the lunch hour. Some people prefer to go round the exhibition then—the place is a bit less crowded.

DAVID: Is there anything else I should bear in mind?

YOUNG: I suggest you bring along your technical dictionaries —just to be on the safe side!

DAVID: Supposing someone turns up whose language neither of us can speak?

YOUNG: In that case, we'll have to use the interpreting service at the Centre. But we'll cross that bridge when we come to it.

DAVID: Why don't we have our catalogues printed in several languages?

YOUNG: That's a very good question! In fact we're working on foreign language versions of our main product catalogue, but unfortunately they aren't going to be ready in time for this exhibition. We ran into a long series of hold-ups—staff leaving, labour disputes at the printers, and so on. The last time I spoke to the head of the printing works, he gave me a delivery date early in November. All we can do is promise the customers to send them a copy as soon as possible. I'm afraid this is one area where we've slipped up rather badly.

Lesson Notes

well up to schedule = according to the programme/plan/time-table. Compare this with *behind schedule* = later than the time stated in the programme etc.
a hitch = a temporary difficulty or set-back
stickers = adhesive labels
to boost = to increase
You won't be left on your own = you won't be left alone
to cope = to manage, to deal successfully with a situation
to come to the rescue = to give help
We'll arrange a rota (for lunch) = We'll arrange to go for lunch in turn
just to be on the safe side = as a precaution (i.e. in case of difficulty)
to turn up = to arrive
We'll cross that bridge when we come to it = We'll consider that problem when and if it arises.

That's a good question! = This is a common response to a slightly difficult or embarrassing question.
to slip up = to make a mistake
We ran into a long series of problems = We experienced a number of problems.

Comprehension

1. Why was David to be included in the team to man the company's stand at the trade fair?
2. Is Mr Young a linguist?
3. Had there been any problems in preparing for the exhibition?
4. Had the problems been dealt with successfully?
5. What aids had the exhibition organizers supplied?
6. How had David prepared himself for his role as interpreter?
7. What was he afraid of?
8. What was his main job at the exhibition to be?
9. Who else was to be on the stand?
10. What was David to try to get from each visitor to the stand? Why?
11. What facilities are there for meals at the Conference Centre?
12. What interpreting facilities are available?
13. Why weren't the foreign language catalogues ready in time for the exhibition?
14. What did Mr Young suggest that David bring to the exhibition with him? Why?

28 An Overseas Visitor

Introduction

The trade fair attracted thousands of visitors, and considerable interest was shown in the Discovery stand. In particular, BI99—the product launched a few weeks previously—attracted much attention and several quite important orders were placed. David was called upon several times to interpret for some of the overseas visitors to the stand, although the majority of such visitors spoke excellent English.

On the second day of the fair, a gentleman who gave his name as Kaye presented his card and asked if it was possible to speak to a Director. Mr Young, the Overseas Director, was on the stand at the time and he invited the visitor into the small reception room on the Discovery stand.

Dialogue

KAYE: Mr Young, I represent Global Engineering. We are, I think, an organization very similar to your own.
YOUNG: I'm very pleased to meet you, Mr Kaye. Please take a seat.
KAYE: Thank you.
YOUNG: Is this your first visit to England?
KAYE: Indeed, no. I was educated here.
YOUNG: That accounts for your excellent English!
KAYE: Thank you.
YOUNG: Have you any representation in England, Mr Kaye?
KAYE: Not directly, although we are developing our exports to your country. As I mentioned, we have much in common with your organization—that is to say, we are both in the field of light engineering and we both sell in the same markets.
YOUNG: May I enquire the nature of your company's products?
KAYE: I have here some of our literature. If you will look at it, I think you will follow my reasoning.
YOUNG: Thank you . . . Yes, I see what you mean. We operate in the same fields—but we're hardly likely to be competitors, are we?
KAYE: I have here a list of some of our major accounts. You may recognize the names.
YOUNG: I certainly do. These are some of OUR biggest customers as well. You've obviously done your homework, Mr Kaye. But you have something else to tell me, I think?

KAYE: Yes, indeed. I come now to the main purpose of my visit. We have recently been developing a device which we believe will arouse considerable interest. Briefly, we think it will significantly improve output in a number of industrial processes.

YOUNG: That sounds interesting.

KAYE: We have carried out surveys which indicate a considerable potential market—although a strong sales effort will be needed to launch the product. We believe the device has novelty, and we wish to derive the maximum advantage from being first in the field.

YOUNG: Naturally.

KAYE: If the predictions of our marketing experts are accurate—and we believe they are—we shall at first have to concentrate on our home market. We do not expect, initially, to be in a position to market the product abroad. In short, we do not have either the production capacity or the sales organization to take full advantage of what we believe is a very promising marketing situation.

YOUNG: And you feel that perhaps this is the time to look for manufacturing facilities elsewhere?

KAYE: Precisely.

YOUNG: Well, Mr Kaye, as it happens we are currently looking into one or two possible additions to our range. We expect to have some spare capacity shortly—a couple of products are being run down—and we might consider some sort of licensing arrangement if we found something suitable.

KAYE: Perhaps, before we go any further, you would like to know something about the product itself?

YOUNG: Indeed I should.

KAYE: Here is a brief write-up and some drawings.

YOUNG: Thank you . . . mm-hm . . . y-e-s . . . that's a common problem no-one seems to have solved satisfactorily . . . mm . . . very ingenious . . . Well now, Mr Kaye, obviously we can't deal with a matter like this in five minutes. In any case, it'll soon be lunch time. Will you be my guest? We can continue our discussion over lunch.

KAYE: With pleasure—that is most kind of you.

Lesson Notes

You've obviously done your homework! = You are obviously well-informed.
first in the field = first to enter the market with a particular product

to look into=to examine, evaluate
to run down a product (in the manufacturing sense)=to reduce output prior to discontinuing it
a write-up=a written description

Grammar

The main point introduced in this Episode is:
65 *either . . . or* and *neither . . . nor*

Comprehension

1 Was the trade fair a success from Discovery Engineering's point of view? Why?
2 How was it that Mr Kaye spoke such good English?
3 Was Global Engineering represented in England?
4 How much did Mr Kaye know about Discovery Engineering?
5 What had Global engineering recently been working on?
6 What did the results of Global Engineering's market survey indicate?
7 What was the purpose of Mr Kaye's visit to the Discovery stand?
8 Why was Global Engineering looking for a licensee in the United Kingdom?
9 What was Mr Young's reaction to Mr Kaye's approach?
10 What did Mr Kaye show him?
11 What interest did Mr Young show in the write-up and drawings?
12 What did Mr Young suggest?
13 What claims did Mr Kaye make for his company's new product?
14 What did Global Engineering and Discovery Engineering have in common?

29 A Business Lunch

Introduction

Mr Young left Mr Kaye in the small reception room on the Discovery stand for a few moments, saying that he wanted to give instructions for a table to be reserved for lunch at his favourite restaurant. He took the opportunity at the same time of asking June Barrett to contact Mr Browning, the Chairman and Managing Director, requesting an urgent meeting during the afternoon. He also told her he would not be returning to the Discovery stand that day. He then returned to his discussion with Mr Kaye, which continued for a further ten minutes before the two men left for lunch.

They went in Mr Young's car to a country restaurant a few miles from the exhibition centre. On arrival, they went to the bar where the head waiter brought them copies of the menu. They gave their order, and over a pre-lunch drink they chatted about matters of general interest until the waiter informed them that their meal was ready. They followed him to the restaurant, which was in an old and historic manor house, and were shown to a table in a secluded corner. During the meal they exchanged some further general background information about their respective companies, and it was not until they had finished eating that the main purpose of their discussion was referred to again.

Dialogue

KAYE: That was an excellent meal, Mr Young—and in a delightful setting. It seems you are a regular visitor here—all the staff appear to know you.
YOUNG: I'm glad you enjoyed it. Yes, it's not a bad place at all. I come here quite often—the food is usually of a pretty high standard.
KAYE: The wine too—congratulations on your choice!
YOUNG: Thank you. Would you care for a liqueur with your coffee? A brandy, perhaps?
KAYE: That would be very pleasant.
YOUNG: Two brandies please, waiter.
WAITER: Certainly, sir.
YOUNG: Cigar, Mr Kaye?
KAYE: No thank you, I never smoke. But please, have one yourself if you wish.
YOUNG: No, that's all right. My wife says I smoke too much

anyway. Now, perhaps we should return to business—by the way, has this product of yours got a name?

KAYE: It has rather a long one in our language—we refer to it by its initials: S.P.O.T.

YOUNG: S.P.O.T.—*Spot*, eh? Well, that's easy for us to remember!

KAYE: And what are your first impressions of—er—*Spot*, Mr Young?

YOUNG: Well, if it'll do what you claim for it, I'd say it has possibilities. You mentioned a market survey—I take it that referred solely to your home market?

KAYE: Yes, but we see no reason why it should not be equally successful abroad.

YOUNG: Now, if I understand you correctly, you are authorized to negotiate with my company terms for the granting of a licence to manufacture and market SPOT in this country.

KAYE: That is correct.

YOUNG: Do you envisage an exclusive licence?

KAYE: Subject to our being satisfied that you have the capacity to meet the demand, we should be prepared to grant you exclusive rights for the whole of the United Kingdom.

YOUNG: Do you intend to grant manufacturing licences in countries other than the UK?

KAYE: That is a possibility, but we might consider granting you selling rights in certain countries.

YOUNG: When do you expect to go into production yourselves?

KAYE: We have almost completed the tooling-up, and we should be in a position to run off the first batch in about a month to six weeks.

YOUNG: Look, Mr Kaye, I believe my Managing Director would be most interested to look into this. I should like to consult him with a view to arranging a full discussion. Where can I contact you?

KAYE: I'm staying at the Castle Hotel—you know it, I expect.

YOUNG: Indeed I do. We hold our annual sales convention there. So—I'll report to my MD and if—as I believe—he wants to have a talk with you himself, I'll be in touch very shortly to suggest a time. How long do you plan to stay in England?

KAYE: I return home at the week-end. I shall be happy to have a call from you and to meet your Managing Director. Now, if you will excuse me, I have an appointment in the city at three o'clock. Would you be kind enough to ask the waiter to order a taxi for me?

YOUNG: By all means—but won't you allow me to give you a lift?

KAYE: I wouldn't dream of putting you to any inconvenience. Thank you all the same.
YOUNG: As you wish. Waiter, the bill please—and will you kindly order a taxi for this gentleman?
WAITER: Certainly, sir ... thank you very much, sir.
KAYE: Well, thank you very much for a delightful lunch, Mr Young. I'll look forward to hearing from you. Good-bye for now.
YOUNG: Good-bye.

Lesson Notes

Would you care for . . . ? = would you like . . . ?
Has this product of yours got a name? This is a further example of the double genitive which first occurred in Episode 25.
I take it . . . = I understand, assume
to go into production = to begin production
to run off the first batch = to produce the first quantity of a new product
to give someone a lift = to drive them to their destination

Comprehension

1 Why did Mr Young leave Mr Kaye alone for a few moments?
2 What instructions did he give to June Barrett?
3 What else did he say to her?
4 Where did the two men go for lunch?
5 Did they discuss Mr Kaye's proposals over lunch?
6 Did Mr Kaye enjoy his lunch?
7 Why did Mr Young refer to the Global Engineering product as SPOT?
8 What was Mr Kaye authorized to do?
9 Did he envisage an exclusive licence?
10 What did he say about selling rights?
11 How soon would Global Engineering be ready to start producing SPOT?
12 What course of action did Mr Young suggest?
13 What was Mr Kaye's reaction to the suggestion?
14 What did he aşk Mr Young to do for him?
15 What further suggestion did Mr Young make?
16 How did Mr Kaye reply?
17 When will the two men meet again?

30 Urgent Discussions

Introduction

As soon as he had parted from Mr Kaye, Mr Young drove straight back to his office and, even before removing his hat and coat, he picked up the telephone and dialled the Managing Director's number. Mr Browning's secretary answered; she had received his message from June Barrett and made an appointment for 3.30. That gave him half-an-hour, which he spent dictating a report on his meeting with Mr Kaye into a dictating machine. Before leaving to keep his appointment he gave the tape to his secretary, asked her to type it as soon as possible and emphasized that it was highly confidential. He also asked her to find out everything she could about Global Engineering.

Dialogue

BROWNING: Sit down, Geoff. What's on your mind? June made it sound pretty urgent.
YOUNG: I think it is. A man called Kaye came to our stand this morning —er, here's his card.
BROWNING: *'Global Engineering'*—can't say it rings any bells. Do you know them?
YOUNG: I've never heard of them before to-day; I've asked Shirley to see what she can unearth on them.
BROWNING: What did he want?
YOUNG: He's looking for someone to make a new product of theirs under licence. They call it SPOT of all things!
BROWNING: I suppose it means something more technical to them, but of course it'd be *Spot* to us.
YOUNG: Yes—well, it's going to put us IN a spot if we're not careful. Do you know what this product is? Or rather, what it does?
BROWNING: Something pretty spectacular to get you steamed up like this, I'd say.
YOUNG: It's a variation on CP21.
BROWNING: You're joking!
YOUNG: I tell you it is. They've taken the same problem that we tackled for—what was the name of those people?
BROWNING: Jones Electronics?
YOUNG: That's the firm. They've worked on that problem, and they've come up with a solution that's uncomfortably close to CP21.
BROWNING: Oh, HAVE they?

YOUNG: And that's not all. He showed me drawings—obviously copies of some prepared for a patent application. They were dated.

BROWNING: Go on—tell me the worst!

YOUNG: They anticipate ours by just one month—I've checked with Stephen Miles's secretary.

BROWNING: Well, this is a difficult one, isn't it? How have you played it so far?

YOUNG: Well, I expressed interest, of course, and said I was sure you'd like to have a talk with him. I let him do most of the talking, although I did let drop that we expect to have some spare capacity soon and are on the look-out for new products.

BROWNING: You didn't say anything about CP21?

YOUNG: Not a word. Obviously, I didn't have the opportunity to study his drawings all that closely, or to make any real comparison with CP21. Anyway, I'm not the technical expert—that'd be a job for R & D. But I'd say that his SPOT was sufficiently close to CP21 to give us quite a lot of trouble.

BROWNING: Have Global started production yet?

YOUNG: No—they're scheduled to start in about six weeks.

BROWNING: And they're talking about overseas licensees already!

YOUNG: Kaye claims the market survey they did shows a big potential, once their sales force has created the demand. I get the impression that they're gambling pretty heavily on being the first in the field.

BROWNING: Well, if that's so, it certainly bears out Tom Blake's forecasts. He's beginning to get some feedback from the test marketing, by the way—in fact, I believe they've asked for another meeting. I think we'd better make it a full Board Meeting—and soon. When are you seeing Kaye again?

YOUNG: I told him I'd try to arrange a meeting with you as soon as possible. He's at the Castle until the week-end—I promised to call him there.

BROWNING: That only gives us a couple of days! Look, we've got to get our heads together quickly and decide what line to take. How soon can you let me have a written report?

YOUNG: It's already on tape—Shirley's working on it now.

BROWNING: Good—if I can have it before she goes home, I'll study it this evening. Make sure there's enough copies to go round, and I'll get everyone together for ten o'clock to-morrow in the Board Room. And bring any information that Shirley has been able to dig out about Global.

YOUNG: Right. See you at ten to-morrow morning.

Lesson Notes

June made it sound pretty urgent=June gave the impression (i.e. from the way she spoke) that the matter was urgent.
Can't say it rings any bells! (coll.)=it doesn't sound familiar. Compare this with *That rings a bell!*=that sounds familiar, reminds me of something I have heard previously.
to put someone in a spot=to cause them difficulty or embarrassment
to get steamed up *(coll.)*=to become agitated or excited
to get another person steamed up *(coll.)*=to cause that person to become excited
to tackle a problem=to take steps to solve it
How have you played it? (coll.)=What attitude have you adopted?
to let drop=to mention during a conversation, without laying much emphasis on the point
to be on the look-out=to be watching or searching for something
I get the impression that they're gambling pretty heavily on being the first in the field=It seems to me that they are investing a lot of money in the project, in the belief that they are the first to launch a product of this nature.
feedback=information received as the result of an enquiry or some other action
We've got to get our heads together (coll.)=we must meet for a discussion.
to decide what line to take=to decide what attitude to adopt, what policy to pursue
Make sure there are enough copies to go round=i.e. one for each person who will be at the meeting.
to dig out ⎱ = to obtain information as the result of a
to unearth ⎰   search or enquiry.

Drills

A David is asking some questions about the trade fair.

Examples

Has our site been booked? (yes, weeks ago)	Yes, it was booked weeks ago.
Has the floor plan come? (no)	No, it hasn't come yet.

Have the salesmen been briefed? (no)

Has our application been posted?
(yes, weeks ago)
Has our stand been designed?
(yes, some time ago)
Has our design been approved?
(yes, last week)
Have the brochures been printed?
(no)
Have the details been finalized?
(no)

B A customer is reading Discovery Engineering's exhibition brochure and reporting to his colleague.

Examples

It is hoped to attract many foreign buyers to the stand.	They hope to attract many foreign buyers to the stand.
Our full range of products is being shown.	They're showing their full range of products.

Any language problems can be dealt with by our interpreter.
Enquiries from new customers will be welcomed.
Our best attention will be given to all orders.
All goods will be delivered as soon as possible.
All complaints will be investigated immediately.

C David has some misgivings about the trade fair.

Examples

The stand may not be ready in time.	Supposing the stand isn't ready in time?
The brochures may not arrive in time.	Supposing the brochures don't arrive in time?
The printers may go on strike.	Supposing the printers go on strike?

I may get an awkward customer.
I may not be able to answer his questions.
I may not be able to speak his language.
The stand may get very crowded.

D A salesman is talking to a prospective customer at the exhibition.

Examples

look at our literature/follow my meaning	If you'll look at our literature, I think you'll follow my meaning.
study our designs/agree good	If you'll study our designs, I think you'll agree they're good.

compare our prices/agree competitive
read the description/understand my arguments
study the performance data/agree satisfactory
compare the products/agree ours better
visit our factory/agree efficient

E A trainee is asking questions about the Company's plans.

Examples

Do you intend to extend the existing factory? (build/new one)	That's a possibility, but we might consider building a new one.
Do you intend to buy new machines? (adapt/existing ones)	That's a possibility, but we might consider adapting the existing ones.

Do you intend to appoint a licensee? (set up/own factory)
Do you intend to recruit more managers? (promote/existing staff)
Do you intend to raise a bank loan? (issue/new shares)
Do you intend to handle your own advertising campaign? (use/agency)

F A sales manager is reassuring a customer.

Examples

have any further questions	If you have any further questions, please get in touch with me.

would like to see the factory   If you'd like to see the
                                  factory, please get in touch
                                  with me.

would like to meet our directors
have any problems
need any technical assistance

Comprehension

1 What did Mr Young do when he arrived back at his office?
2 What instructions did he give his secretary?
3 Why was SPOT likely to cause problems for Discovery Engineering?
4 What was significant about the date on the Global Engineering drawings?
5 When did Global Engineering expect to start production?
6 Why were they seeking a licensee at such an early stage?
7 What was the existing position regarding CP21?
8 How long did Mr Kaye plan to remain in England?
9 When did Mr Browning want the written report?
10 When did he intend to arrange the Board Meeting?
11 What did he intend to do that evening?
12 What final instructions did Mr Browning give Mr Young?

31 The Board Meeting

Introduction

Following his discussion with the Overseas Director, Mr Browning telephoned all the other directors of Discovery Engineering, asking them to attend an emergency Board meeting the following morning. Apart from the minutes of the previous meeting and any matters arising, there was to be a single item on the agenda, namely the proposal made by Mr Kaye on behalf of Global Engineering and its probable effect on the future of CP21.

Just after 5.30 that evening, Mr Young's secretary delivered the report on his meeting with Mr Kaye, together with a note of all that she had been able to find out about Global. Mr Browning took both these home with him. He also put into his briefcase a copy of Discovery's own patent specification on CP21.

At ten o'clock the next day, all seven directors assembled in the Board Room. They were:

James Browning (Chairman and Managing Director)
Stephen Miles (Financial Director and Company Secretary)
Richard Simpson (non-Executive Director)
Thomas Blake (Sales and Marketing Director)
Geoffrey Young (Overseas Director)
William Pound (Manufacturing Director)
Michael Green (Management Services Director)

Mr Browning opened the meeting by asking Mr Miles to read the minutes of the previous Board meeting. There were one or two matters arising from the minutes, which were quickly dealt with, and then Mr Browning moved on to the purpose for which the meeting had been called.

Dialogue

BROWNING: Can I take it that you've all had an opportunity to run through Geoff's report on his meeting with Mr Kaye of Global Engineering?
All: Yes . . . yes . . . mmm . . .
BROWNING: So you all know the situation. Now, I spent quite a bit of time thinking about this last night, and I'll tell you my thoughts later on when you've all had a chance to state your own views. Tom, I'm going to ask you first of all to tell us what sort of results you've had from your test marketing of CP21.
BLAKE: Well, you've caught me on the hop, as a matter of

fact—I hadn't finished analysing all the reports when you telephoned yesterday. I've done this rough summary—I'm sorry there wasn't time to get it typed. Anyway, on the basis of what we've done so far, I'd say there's been enough positive interest shown to justify going ahead.

BROWNING: Thank you, that's fine. Now, let's assume for a moment that Global had gone to someone else with SPOT and that we'd started producing CP21 in all good faith without knowing anything about it. What would happen then?

BLAKE: Well, we'd have a few months' start on the competition—but equally, they'd be bound to reap some benefit from our sales efforts. And if our product IS as close to theirs as Geoff seems to think, we'd be in trouble over the patent situation sooner or later.

BROWNING: Bill, what do you think about the patent aspect?

POUND: Without seeing at least a drawing of SPOT, I can't be sure how close it is to CP21. And without seeing the Global patent specification—which of course is out of the question at the moment—I can't say whether CP21 infringes it or not. Anyway, this is pure speculation; neither of us has a patent yet, and won't have one for many months at the very least.

YOUNG: May I say something, JB?

BROWNING: Of course, Geoff. Go ahead.

YOUNG: It seems to me we've got to decide on wider issues than possible patent infringements. If it came to a dispute, litigation costs the earth and—even if we won—we could easily end up paying out a substantial portion of our profits on CP21 in legal fees.

BROWNING: True. Go on.

YOUNG: As I see it, there's a whole new market waiting to be exploited, and the first one in is going to have a big advantage. Tom's test marketing bears out what Global's own market survey told them—the potential is there. If we enter the field as Global's competitor—leaving aside the problematical question of patents—we shall be cutting each other's throats, and our profit margins. If we join forces, we'll both be better off.

BROWNING: I take it, then, that you are in favour of laying our cards on the table?

YOUNG: Yes, I am. I think we should be quite straightforward and say: Look, we can either do each other a lot of good, or we can do each other a lot of harm. Let's get together and get the greatest possible benefit from our mutual know-how.

BROWNING: Thanks, Geoff. Tom, do you go along with that?

BLAKE: When you say: cards on the table, I take it you mean showing Kaye CP21?

BROWNING: I can't see any reason why not.
BLAKE: I suppose not. OK then—yes, I'm with Geoff.
BROWNING: What do you say, Dick?
SIMPSON: It occurs to me that until we can scrutinize SPOT and its patent claims in detail, we can't be certain that WE haven't got something to bargain with.
BLAKE: I can't see how—if their patent application anticipates ours.
SIMPSON: Our product may have features that they haven't thought of. Any such features would be protected by our own patent application. In any case, there's no guarantee that either of us is going to get a patent.
BLAKE: But the idea's completely new!
SIMPSON: It's new in this field—yes. But for all we know someone may have thought of it years ago for some totally different use, and patented it. There are hundreds of thousands of patents in existence—it's getting more difficult every year to prove that an invention has novelty.
BROWNING: We're losing sight of the main question, gentlemen. Are we, or are we not, going to come clean with Global and try to work out something to our mutual advantage? Stephen, you haven't said anything yet.
MILES: From the purely financial point of view I can see certain advantages in joining forces with Global. If we can agree on the terms of the licensing agreement, that is. The fact that we already have considerable know-how in this field should count for something. On the whole I'm in favour of opening discussions immediately. After all, if we shilly-shally there's always the chance that Global will approach someone else.
BROWNING: What about you, Mike? Do you think we should tell Kaye about CP21?
GREEN: Yes, I do—for ethical as well as commercial reasons. I can foresee nothing but complications if we keep quiet. I'm all for having Kaye over here at the earliest possible moment, telling him frankly what the situation is, and taking it from there. I can see from Geoff's report that Global is in a fair way of business—what was your impression of Kaye personally, Geoff?
YOUNG: Very favourable. I'd say he's completely genuine.
BROWNING: Very well, gentlemen. It seems we have a consensus. I came to the same conclusion myself last night. I therefore move that we invite Kaye along and open discussions right away. All in favour?
ALL: Yes . . . agreed . . .
BROWNING: Carried unanimously.

Lesson Notes

to run through=to read quickly
quite a bit of time=a considerable time
You've caught me on the hop (coll.)=I was unprepared, I wasn't ready
in all good faith=without any dishonourable intention
to have a start on someone=to have an advantage by beginning earlier
out of the question=impossible, impracticable
if it came to a dispute=if we became involved in a dispute
litigation costs the earth (coll.)=litigation is very expensive
we shall be cutting each other's throats=we shall be doing each other harm
to cut one's profits=to reduce one's profits
to lay one's cards on the table=to reveal one's plans frankly
know-how=technical and commercial knowledge, expertise
to go along with (a decision, an argument)=to accept, agree with
to come clean (*coll.*)=to admit, to be frank
purely=exclusively
to shilly-shally=to hesitate, prevaricate
I'm all for . . .=I am strongly in favour of . . .
in a fair way of business=substantial, considerable

Comprehension

1 What was on the agenda for the Board Meeting?
2 What did Mr Browning take home with him?
3 How did the Board Meeting open?
4 What did Mr Blake report about the test marketing of CP21?
5 Why could he only show a rough summary of the results?
6 What did Mr Blake suggest would happen, if Discovery went ahead without any knowledge of SPOT?
7 What did Mr Pound think about the patent situation?
8 What was Mr Young's attitude to the patent question?
9 What action did Mr Young favour?
10 Did Mr Blake agree immediately with the suggestion put forward by Mr Young?
11 What point did Mr Simpson raise?
12 Why did Mr Simpson think that there was some doubt whether Discovery would get a patent for CP21?

13 What advantage did Mr Miles see in joining forces with Global Engineering?
14 What possibility did he envisage if Discovery hesitated?
15 What view did Mr Green take of the situation?
16 What conclusions did the meeting reach?
17 Was it a unanimous decision?

32 Consultations

Introduction

Having agreed in principle on their attitude to Global Engineering's proposals, the directors of Discovery Engineering proceeded to consider detailed arrangements for a meeting with Mr Kaye. After some discussion, it was decided to try to arrange the first formal meeting for the following morning. Mr Miles was asked to draw up a list of possible headings to be used as the basis for a draft agreement. Mr Blake would complete his report on the test marketing of CP21 and have it typed. Mr Pound would check with John Edwards, the Product Manager for CP21, to make sure that he had all the data at his fingertips; he would also arrange for an engineer from R & D to be available to attend the meeting in case any technical queries arose. Finally, it was settled that Mr Browning and Mr Young should invite Mr Kaye to dinner that evening, with the object of telling him frankly about CP21 and of having a preliminary, informal talk about the whole affair.

It was not until fairly late that afternoon that they were able to reach Mr Kaye at his hotel, but when Mr Browning's secretary eventually contacted him, he accepted the joint invitation to dinner without hesitation. Before setting out for the hotel to meet him, the two Discovery directors discussed what their approach should be.

Dialogue

YOUNG: I must say, this is a situation I haven't come up against before. Have you decided exactly how you're going to broach the subject?

BROWNING: More or less. I don't intend to beat about the bush or waste half the evening on small talk. I propose—after the usual preliminaries—to come straight to the point. What are your feelings?

YOUNG: I certainly think that's the best course to adopt. If we wait until the evening's half over and then spring it on him, he's bound to feel at a disadvantage.

BROWNING: Yes—he might think we'd been trying to get him to spill as much as possible before showing our hand. You'll leave it to me to raise the subject?

YOUNG: Agreed. I'll take my cue from you.

BROWNING: Now, to look ahead a bit farther. I must admit

I'm not so clear in my mind about the next stage. There are several big question marks.

YOUNG: Such as: does CP21 infringe their patent claims? Does SPOT infringe any of ours?

BROWNING: To name but two! By the way, have you anything to add to the information you gave me on Global?

YOUNG: Yes, as a matter of fact I have. The details Shirley gave you last night were just taken from a trade directory. This morning I got her to do a bit of detective work. We don't have an agent on the spot but we do have one in a neighbouring country. We telexed him to see what he could find. The reply came back late this afternoon; here it is.

BROWNING: Thanks. I see . . . mm hm . . . well, it seems they're pretty sound and well thought of. About the same size of company as Discovery.

YOUNG: I'm sure this is a bona fide proposal that Kaye is making.

BROWNING: Yes, I'm sure it is. We'll do the normal trade and bankers' references of course, as a routine measure; no doubt they'll do the same on us.

YOUNG: They've probably done so already!

BROWNING: Probably. Anyway, to get back to this evening. A lot will depend on how Kaye reacts to our news, of course, but assuming that he's genuinely anxious to get SPOT launched in the British market as soon as possible, I can't see any reason why it should put him off.

YOUNG: He may want to consult his fellow directors before going any further.

BROWNING: Well, he'll have the chance to do that before to-morrow's meeting. That's another advantage of breaking it to him this evening. He'll have plenty of time to think things over and decide what line he's going to take. Anyway, it's time we were leaving. Is there anything else we need to talk about before meeting Kaye?

YOUNG: No, I don't think so. What time did you say we'd pick him up?

BROWNING: Seven-thirty. Do you mind if we use your car? Mine's in for service.

YOUNG: Of course—I was going to suggest it.

BROWNING: Thanks. Let's be on our way.

Lesson Notes

to have something at one's fingertips = to be thoroughly familiar with all the essential facts about it

to reach someone = to make contact with them (for example, by telephone)
to come up against (a situation) = to experience
to beat about the bush = to approach a subject indirectly
to spring something on someone = to act or speak without prior hint or warning.
he's bound to ... = he'll be certain to ..., it is certain that he will ...
to spill (information) = to reveal, to give away (compare: to let drop, Episode 30)
to show one's hand = to reveal one's intentions
I'll take my cue from you = I'll wait for you to raise the matter and then join in the conversation in a suitable way.
on the spot = in the exact place, the same country
I got her to do a bit of detective work = I asked her to make searching enquiries.
I can't see any reason why it should put him off = I see no reason why it should cause him to lose interest.
to pick someone up = to call for them at a pre-arranged place, with the object of going to a common destination
My car's in for service = my car is at the garage for routine maintenance.

Comprehension

1 When did the Discovery directors hope to arrange the first formal meeting with Mr Kaye?
2 What was Mr Miles asked to do?
3 What was Mr Pound going to speak to John Edwards about?
4 What else was Mr Pound going to arrange?
5 What were Mr Young and Mr Browning going to do before the proposed formal meeting?
6 What was the main purpose of having an informal discussion over dinner?
7 What approach did Browning and Young agree on? Why?
8 What further information did Shirley obtain about Global Engineering?
9 Did the Discovery directors believe that Mr Kaye's proposal was genuine?
10 What further enquiries were they going to make about Global Engineering?
11 What were the advantages of breaking the news of CP21 to Mr Kaye in advance of the formal meeting?
12 Why did the two Discovery directors go out in Mr Young's car?

33 Negotiations

Introduction

When Mr Browning and Mr Young arrived at the Castle Hotel they found their guest waiting for them in reception. He immediately got up to greet them, and Mr Young performed the introductions. The three men then drove to a nearby restaurant where a table had been reserved for eight o'clock. They went first to the lounge and sat down in an alcove by the fire. They ordered drinks, and the conversation very soon turned to the main purpose of their meeting.

Dialogue

KAYE: The thing I enjoy most about England in the autumn is a log fire!

BROWNING: Yes, it's very cosy, isn't it? Central heating is convenient, of course, but an open fire does make a place look cheerful.

YOUNG: What sort of a day have you had, Mr Kaye?

KAYE: Very pleasant, thank you. I visited one or two customers this morning; this afternoon I had another look round the exhibition.

BROWNING:. What do you think of our new exhibition centre?

KAYE: It is most impressive. The fair itself is also very interesting. I intend to recommend that we participate next year.

BROWNING: If by that time our two companies are associated, we might consider a joint exhibit, perhaps?

KAYE: That is a most interesting suggestion. May I take it that you are interested in an association?

BROWNING: In principle, yes, Mr Kaye. We're very interested. There is, however, something you should know before we go any further.

KAYE: Oh—what is that?

BROWNING: As you yourself said to Mr Young yesterday, your company and ours have much in common. We sell, in many cases, to the same customers, and our customers have similar problems to yours. Sometimes they bring their problems to us to solve, and we do our best to help them. No doubt you have similar experiences.

KAYE: Naturally. That is the kind of situation which led us to develop SPOT.

BROWNING: Exactly. And, Mr Kaye, by a coincidence, the same thing happened to us. We too have produced a device to handle this kind of problem, and Mr Young tells me that it is in many respects similar to SPOT.

KAYE: But this is most extraordinary! Excuse me, Mr Young, but why did you not mention this to me yesterday?

YOUNG: Mr Kaye, CP21 hasn't yet been launched—in fact, we've only just finished our own market research. I could hardly reveal anything without first consulting my Managing Director.

KAYE: Yes, I understand. You were in a somewhat embarrassing position.

BROWNING: Mr Young reported back to me immediately he left you yesterday and my fellow directors and I considered the affair very seriously. We decided unanimously to take you into our confidence, as a sign of our good faith.

KAYE: I appreciate that. It seems our negotiations will follow a somewhat unexpected course, from my company's point of view.

BROWNING: Before we go any further, Mr Kaye, I have in my briefcase a drawing of CP21. You didn't by any chance bring your drawings with you? It would be interesting to compare them.

KAYE: Yes, indeed. I have the papers here.

BROWNING: Splendid. Let's have a look at them ... Geoff, how about another round?

YOUNG: Of course. The same again, Mr Kaye?

KAYE: Thank you.

YOUNG: And for you, JB?

BROWNING: Yes, please.

YOUNG: Waiter! Three large whiskies please.

WAITER: Yes sir. Would you like to order dinner now, sir?

YOUNG: Not just yet. In about fifteen minutes.

WAITER: Very good, sir ... your drinks, sir.

YOUNG: Thank you ... Here we are! Well, what's the verdict? Are we on to a winner?

KAYE: This is certainly a most interesting situation. Our designs follow one another very closely in the main, but there are some significant differences.

BROWNING: There's no doubt that the basic principle is the same, but we shall need to consider the pros and cons of the features which differ.

KAYE: Are you implying that we should combine our two designs, taking the best features of each?

BROWNING: That strikes me as a reasonable basis for discussion. Do you agree?

KAYE: Well ... I'm not sure ... perhaps ...

YOUNG: If I may say so, it seems to me that the situation has tremendous opportunities for both of us. As far as we know,

there's no-one else in the market so far. But once we start, there'll soon be imitators, trying to get round our patents and cash in on our sales efforts. Surely, it's sensible to pool our resources and our know-how, to get the best possible start on the competition and maintain our lead.
KAYE: That would certainly be preferable to a competitive situation at the outset.
BROWNING: Of course it would. Let's drink to our future association!
YOUNG: Waiter, we'd like to order dinner now.
WAITER: Yes sir. Here's the menu.

Lesson Notes

cosy = comfortable, intimate
... *why did you not mention this to me yesterday?* Mr Kaye is a foreigner and is speaking very correctly, using the full form of 'not' in this sentence (see Grammar Note 8[g]). This affects the word order; an Englishman would say: ... *why didn't you ...?*
a round (of drinks) = a drink for each member of the party
pros and cons = arguments in favour (pros) and against (cons)
... *imitators trying to get round our patents* ... = trying to achieve the same result without infringing our patents
... *and cash in on our sales efforts.* = and benefit from the work we have done to create a market
to pool one's resources = to exchange all relevant information and expertise

Comprehension

1 What did Mr Kaye comment on when the three men arrived at the restaurant?
2 How had Mr Kaye spent the day?
3 What was his impression of the exhibition centre?
4 What did he say about the trade fair itself?
5 What suggestion did Mr Browning make? What was Mr Kaye's reaction to this?
6 How did Mr Browning lead into the subject of the similarity of the two companies' products?
7 What was Mr Kaye's first reaction to the news?
8 How did Mr Young explain his failure to mention CP21?
9 Did Mr Kaye accept his explanation?
10 What did a comparison of the two products show?
11 How was it suggested the situation be tackled?
12 Did Mr Kaye accept the suggestion at once?
13 What arguments did Mr Young use to persuade him?
14 Did those arguments succeed?

34 The Secretary's Department – One

Introduction

The first formal meeting between Mr Kaye and the Discovery directors began, as arranged, at eleven o'clock the following morning. In the meantime, however, Mr Kaye had contacted his head office by telephone and spoken to the head of Global Engineering, who was naturally surprised at the unexpected development. He accepted in principle the idea of pooling know-how with Discovery, but said he would like to send a design engineer to England to take part in the negotiations. Mr Kaye therefore delayed his return home and asked for a further meeting. This was arranged for the following Monday; it lasted all day and at the end of it, agreement had been reached on all essential points. A list of heads of agreement was prepared and signed by both parties, and the meeting ended on a very cordial and optimistic note.

A few days later, Mr Green telephoned Mr Miles, the Company Secretary, and mentioned that it was time for the two management trainees, Sheila Smith and David Long, to gain further experience. Mr Miles agreed that the former could join his department for a few weeks. When she arrived, he spent a little time with her, explaining the principal functions of his department.

Dialogue

MILES: Have you any idea what a Company Secretary's responsibilities are, Miss Smith?

SHEILA: Not really, I'm afraid, except that you attend Board Meetings and take the minutes.

MILES: That's just one of my functions. Briefly, my main responsibility is to ensure that all statutory requirements are fulfilled by the company. In other words, that the company obeys the law, and particularly the Companies Acts.

SHEILA: What does that involve?

MILES: Such things as the keeping of proper accounts, the filing of returns, recording share transactions, maintaining a register of sealed documents and keeping the seal itself in safe custody.

SHEILA: What is the seal?

MILES: It's the equivalent of the Company's signature on a document. It may only be affixed in accordance with the Articles of Association.

SHEILA: What does that mean?

MILES: When a company is formed, it has a Memorandum and Articles of Association. The Memorandum of Association sets out the objects for which the company is formed—for example, to make cars, or build houses or drill for oil. The company may do nothing that isn't covered by the objects clause in the Memorandum. The Articles of Association set out the way the company is to be run—how many directors it may have, how often they must meet, how many shareholders there may be, who must attest the seal, and so on.

SHEILA: Where is the seal kept?

MILES: In the safe in this office, along with the Minute Book, the Share Registers and other important company records.

SHEILA: You mentioned accounts. Doesn't the Chief Accountant look after those?

MILES: He's responsible for the day-to-day running of the Accounts Department but the Company Secretary is responsible for the proper accounts and accounting records being kept and a Balance Sheet and Profit and Loss Account being prepared each year.

SHEILA: What else goes on in the department?

MILES: Well, we try to maintain an information service on any aspect of law which affects the Company in any way. For example, if it is decided to lease new premises, we check the terms of the lease and, if necessary, consult our solicitor on any points we aren't happy about. Then, we advise on commercial agreements. If the factory wants to hire a new item of plant, we vet the proposed contract of hire to make sure that the terms are acceptable.

SHEILA: What's in all these filing cabinets?

MILES: The top drawer contains patent documents. We keep records in this office of all matters relating to patents, trade marks and registered designs. The second drawer down contains all the documents and correspondence relating to our insurances.

SHEILA: Do you have to handle insurance matters as well?

MILES: Our Insurance Manager handles most of it, and his secretary looks after the routine and clerical work. But he is responsible to me, and I am responsible to the Board.

SHEILA: But you're on the Board yourself, aren't you?

MILES: Yes, I'm the Financial Director.

SHEILA: What does that involve?

MILES: Look, I think I've told you enough to be going on with. There's a limit to the amount of information you can take in at one go.

SHEILA: That's quite true. Anyway, I expect you've got plenty of other things to do besides answering my questions.

MILES: I suggest you go and have a talk with my assistant, Marion Clark. She'll be glad of your help this morning, as a matter of fact. I've asked her to bring our schedule of office machinery up to date, and she's finding it rather heavy going. I must get back to this draft agreement with Global.
SHEILA: All right—I'll go and make myself useful.

Lesson Notes

The company may do nothing ... This is more formal, and slightly more emphatic, than: 'the company may not do anything ...'
... how many directors it may have ... =how many directors it is permitted to have
... how often they must meet ... =how often they are obliged to meet
to vet (a document) *(coll.)*=to scrutinize it for errors or unacceptable conditions
enough to be going on with=enough for present needs
at one go=in one lesson, at one single attempt
heavy going *(coll.)*=difficult, troublesome, time-consuming
heads of agreement=a legal term which either means a very short form of agreement, or a list of headings under which agreement has been or will be reached, and which will eventually form the basis of a detailed contract.

Comprehension

1 What is the main responsibility of a Company Secretary?
2 What is the function of a company's seal?
3 What is the Memorandum of Association of a company?
4 What are the Articles of Association?
5 What is the Chief Accountant responsible for?
6 What type of service does the Company Secretary's department give to other departments?
7 Who handles insurance at Discovery Engineering?
8 Who is the Insurance Manager responsible to?
9 What task (in the episode) was Marion Clark engaged on?
10 Why would she be glad of Sheila's help?
11 Why wouldn't Mr Miles answer any more of Sheila's questions?
12 What did he have to get back to?

35 The Secretary's Department – Two

Introduction

Marion Clark was Mr Miles's personal assistant. She handled a great deal of the administrative work of the department and her duties brought her into contact with practically every other department of the company. The Secretary's department maintained records of all the company's plant and machinery, both in the factory and in the offices. This was partly for insurance purposes and partly so that the value of such assets could be shown in the accounts. Marion was currently checking the schedule of office machinery—typewriters, duplicators, copying machines, dictating machines, calculators and so forth. Every time a new piece of equipment was purchased the Secretary's department had to be informed so that it could be added to the schedule. Separate records were kept of items on hire, such as accounting and data processing machines, certain plant in the factory, and the company cars and delivery vehicles.

Owing to pressure of work, Marion was having difficulty in finding the time to go round the departments to check her records and she was very glad of some help. Sheila spent most of the morning visiting the various offices and checking items against the schedule. It was getting on for lunch time when she returned to the office.

Dialogue

MARION: Ah, there you are! How did you get on?

SHEILA: I can understand why you need to check these on the spot—it must be the only way to keep track of them.

MARION: Why—did you have problems?

SHEILA: Well, quite a few items have found their way into different offices from the ones on the list.

MARION: I'm not surprised—they often swap machines around without saying anything to us. It's very naughty of them but we can't stop them.

SHEILA: I've managed to track down most of the items, but there are one or two discrepancies. The electric typewriters are all OK—I've ticked them off—but there's a manual one missing from Personnel. There's an extra one in the stores but its serial number doesn't appear on the list.

MARION: We may find it's a machine that's on loan to us while one of ours is being repaired.

SHEILA: Do we have a maintenance contract for typewriters?

MARION: We used to, but someone did a costing exercise and decided it'd be cheaper to train all the typists to do routine cleaning and oiling, and only call in a mechanic when a machine actually broke down. So we terminated the agreement.

SHEILA: And did it work out cheaper?

MARION: It's too soon to say. We're supposed to be doing it for a trial period of two years, and then the whole question will be reviewed again.

SHEILA: Well, that's the typewriter schedule; here's the one for calculators. The desk models are OK but there seem to be several small ones missing. I couldn't do much about them because the people who are supposed to have them aren't in to-day.

MARION: I expect they've taken them home to work out their income tax! Let me have a note of them and I'll have a word with the people concerned.

SHEILA: I didn't make much progress with the dictating machines, I'm afraid.

MARION: They're always a headache—people cart them around to use in their cars or do work in the evenings. I usually send a note round to all the people on the list, asking them to check the serial numbers and confirm that they still have the machines.

SHEILA: That sounds like a job for me. Shall I type the notes this afternoon?

MARION: Thanks, that'd be a great help.

SHEILA: What happens about the big accounting machines—don't you keep a schedule of those?

MARION: Yes, but they're on hire from the manufacturers. The agreements are kept in that filing cabinet over there under *Plant and Machinery Hire*.

SHEILA: Why do we hire machines instead of buying them?

MARION: There are a number of reasons. For example, technology develops so fast that improvements are continually being made. Leasing the equipment instead of buying it enables us to have the most up-to-date installation at all times. Also, the cost is spread out instead of the company having to invest large sums in capital items.

SHEILA: But surely, we pay the same amount in the end—more in fact?

MARION: Well, I don't really understand all the pros and cons. It's just the company policy to do it this way.

Lesson Notes

to keep track of something=to keep a record of its movements
Quite a few items have found their way into different offices=a number of items are in different offices without a record being made
to swap *(coll.)*=to exchange
to track down=to find something as the result of searching or making enquiries
to tick off (items on a list)=to mark with a tick after checking
They're always a headache (coll.)=they always cause problems
to cart *(coll.)*=to carry

Grammar

The main point introduced in this Episode is:
66   *used to* + infinitive

Drills

A

Examples

You haven't seen my briefcase, have you? (on the desk)	Yes, as a matter of fact I have—it's on the desk.
You don't by any chance know where the Chairman is, do you? (in the Boardroom)	Yes, as a matter of fact I do—he's in the Boardroom.

I don't suppose you've seen Sheila, have you? (in the canteen)
We don't lease this machinery, do we? (works out cheaper)
You haven't got a technical dictionary, have you? (in the bookcase)
Are you by any chance going into town at lunch-time? (want a lift?)

B

Examples

John Edwards is in the Marketing Department, isn't he? (Production Department)	No, as a matter of fact he's in the Production Department.
Sheila's a secretary, I believe? (management trainee)	No, as a matter of fact she's a management trainee.

Of course, Mrs Wood is in charge of wages, isn't she? (advertising)
Am I right in thinking to-day is early closing day? (to-morrow)
I understand we hold the sales convention at the King's Head Hotel. (Castle Hotel)
Is it true that Sheila is moving to the Overseas Department? (Secretary's department)

C

Examples

England in autumn/log fire	The thing I like best about England in the autumn is a log fire.
Switzerland in winter/skiing	The thing I like best about Switzerland in winter is the skiing.

Germany in the autumn/beer festivals
a holiday in Scotland/scenery
a trip to Paris/food
a visit to Milan/opera

D

Examples

We'd better get up early or we'll miss the train.	Yes, if we don't get up early we're bound to miss it.
Ruth will have to work hard, or she'll fail her exams.	Yes, if she doesn't work hard, she's bound to fail them.

Sheila must be careful not to lose track of the machines.
David ought to take his dictionaries, in case he needs them.
I must make a shopping list, in case I forget something.
I'm going to take my umbrella; they say it's going to rain.

E

Examples

Speak to Chairman/not decided what to do	I managed to speak to the Chairman, but he still hasn't decided what to do.
Contact the printers/not sent proofs	I managed to contact the printers, but they still haven't sent the proofs.

See the buyer/not placed order
Speak to the mechanic/not repaired car
Get through to the distributor/not received goods
Talk to the hotel/not seen Mr Kaye

F

Examples

Do we have a maintenance contract for typewriters?	Not now, but we used to have one.
Do we hire the salesmen's cars?	Not now, but we used to hire them.

Does David live in London?
Does Mrs Wood drive a car?
Is the Discovery Head Office in London?
Is Sheila in the Marketing Department?

Comprehension

1 What work did Marion Clark handle?
2 Why did the Secretary's department keep a schedule of plant and machinery?
3 What was Marion checking?
4 Why was she finding it difficult to do the job?
5 Why was she glad that Sheila had come to the department?
6 How did Marion account for the extra machine in the stores?
7 Was there a maintenance contract for the typewriters?

8 Why was it decided to terminate the maintenance agreement?
9 When would the question be reviewed again?
10 How did Marion usually check the dictating machines?
11 What reasons did Marion give for the company's hiring machinery instead of buying it?
12 What point did Sheila raise?

36 The Draft Agreement

Introduction

While Sheila was working on the schedules of office machinery, Mr Miles was discussing with Marion Clark the draft agreement with Global Engineering. The fact that both parties to the agreement had applied for patents was a complication which called for very careful wording of the document, and it would be necessary to obtain advice from both the Company's solicitor and Patent Agent. Mr Miles also thought it advisable to consult an overseas lawyer in order to check on any possible restrictions likely to be imposed locally. Accordingly, he asked Marion to write to the Commercial Attaché at the British Embassy to ask for advice on this point.

Because of the patent situation, both parties had accepted the principle of a cross-licensing agreement, with a separate contract to cover the exchange of know-how. A great deal of typing was involved and Marion asked Sheila to help.

Dialogue

MARION: How are you getting on with the schedules?
SHEILA: I've almost finished them—I just have one or two more notes to type. Have you anything else for me to do?
MARION: Mr Miles wants this draft agreement typed as soon as possible. He wants our solicitor and our patent agent to have a look at it. He also wants it checked by a local lawyer.
SHEILA: What's the reason for that?
MARION: It's as well to know of any special provisions that may affect the agreement. It's particularly important when it comes to transferring licence fees—there are often Government restrictions on sending money overseas.
SHEILA: Let me see if I understand what's happening. Global and Discovery have each invented a device to perform a certain job. The two things are very similar. Global got in first with their patent application, but they think some features of our product are better than theirs. So they're going to let us use their patent and we're going to let them use ours. Is that right?
MARION: Broadly speaking, yes.
SHEILA: How will they fix the licence fees?
MARION: It's already been agreed in principle to apportion the value of the patents. Global won't receive so much in the way of fees as it would have done, had Discovery not developed its

own product. But of course, if Global hadn't come on the scene, Discovery wouldn't have had to pay any fees at all.
SHEILA: So really this isn't a very good thing for us?
MARION: I don't think it's altogether a bad thing. We benefit from an exchange of know-how, and the two companies together will probably be able to exploit the invention more effectively over a wider territory than one on its own.
SHEILA: In other words, if you can't beat 'em, join 'em!
MARION: Exactly!
SHEILA: Everyone's talking about patent applications. How long before we actually get a patent?
MARION: That depends on what the Examiner finds when he studies our specification. He may cite previous patents and suggest that they anticipate our claims.
SHEILA: What happens then?
MARION: The people in R & D get their heads together and try to answer the Examiner's objections.
SHEILA: I imagine this can take a long time.
MARION: It can take up to two-and-a-half years in this country. But once the application is accepted, the patent dates from the date of filing the complete specification. The details vary from country to country, of course.
SHEILA: And meanwhile we put *Patents Pending* on the sales literature?
MARION: That's right—you're learning!
SHEILA: Now, what do you want me to do?
MARION: Well, this draft has been based on an existing agreement with one of our licensees, but of course Mr Miles has made a lot of alterations. He wants a copy for our solicitor, one for our patent again, one for the Overseas lawyer (when we find one) and one for our own files. That's one plus three.
SHEILA: What about Global—don't they get one?
MARION: Not at this stage—not until the legal people have approved our draft.
SHEILA: I see. Shall I use this manual machine or can I borrow your electric one?
MARION: I shall be using mine—I thought we'd type half each. But you ought to have an electric one—it'll take you ages on a manual. I'll see if we can borrow one from Accounts.
SHEILA: We must make sure it goes back—I don't want my schedule upset so soon!

Lesson Notes

a cross-licensing agreement = an agreement under which each party agrees to grant a licence to the other.
it's as well = it's advisable
Global got in first with their patent application = Global filed their patent application before Discovery filed theirs.
If you can't beat 'em, join 'em! = It's better to work together than to engage in a war that neither side can win.
one plus three = one original and three carbon copies (of a typewritten document)
It'll take ages = it will take a long time.

Comprehension

1. Why was the agreement between Discovery and Global going to need very careful wording?
2. Why was Marion going to write to the Commercial Attaché at the British Embassy?
3. What type of licensing agreement was envisaged?
4. Who was the draft agreement going to be sent to?
5. Why was the draft to be checked by a local lawyer?
6. What was the exact situation with regard to the two companies' patents?
7. How were the fees going to be fixed?
8. How did the two companies hope to benefit from the arrangement?
9. How are patent applications dealt with by the British Examiner?
10. How are the Examiner's objections dealt with at Discovery Engineering?
11. Does it take a long time for a patent to be granted?
12. What wording can be used to indicate that a patent application has been filed?

37 Insurance

Introduction

Sheila found the work of the Secretary's department very interesting and took every opportunity of increasing her knowledge. One day, the Insurance Manager's secretary was away ill and Sheila was asked to deputize for her. The Insurance Manager's name was Mr Glyn; he worked in a small room separated from the main office by a glazed partition. He was more than ready to answer Sheila's questions about his work.

Dialogue

GLYN: It's very kind of you to stand in for my secretary, Miss Smith. I'm quite lost without someone to do my typing for me.
SHEILA: That's quite all right. I hope there's nothing seriously wrong with her.
GLYN: Just a touch of 'flu, I think. She hopes to be back next week.
SHEILA: Well, I'll do my best to help, but I'm afraid I don't know a great deal about insurance.
GLYN: I've got some letters here that need attention—I've put the replies on this tape. Can you use a dictating machine?
SHEILA: Yes.
GLYN: Good. Don't hesitate to ask me if you have any queries.
SHEILA: May I ask you a few questions before I start typing?
GLYN: By all means—go ahead.
SHEILA: First of all—how many different types of insurance are there?
GLYN: That's a tall one! Let's see now—the buildings. They have to be insured against fire, flood, tempest and other perils. Similar cover has to be arranged on the contents—office furniture, books, equipment and so on.
SHEILA: What about the factory—the plant and machinery, for example?
GLYN: The heavy plant is covered by special engineering insurance. We're also covered against consequential loss, and loss of profits.
SHEILA: What's *consequential loss*?
GLYN: Suppose one of our delivery vehicles catches fire and the load is destroyed. We claim for the value of the goods under our *Goods in Transit* cover. But if, because we can't replace the lost goods quickly enough, we lose valuable orders,

our loss is much greater than the value of the goods destroyed by the fire. That's an example of consequential loss.

SHEILA: What about *loss of profits* insurance?

GLYN: That's a special cover we arrange in case we have to suspend operations because all or part of our premises are put out of action by fire or some other disaster. Again, the loss to the company would be much greater than the value of the buildings and equipment destroyed or damaged.

SHEILA: I see. What other types of insurance are there?

GLYN: Well, there's *Public Liability* insurance. If a member of the public is injured whilst on our premises, or through the negligence of one of our employees, that person may claim damages from us.

SHEILA: When you say *member of the public*, does that include the employees?

GLYN: No. Our *Employer's Liability* insurance takes care of them.

SHEILA: What about theft, burglary and so on?

GLYN: Yes, we're covered against all kinds of theft, both on the premises and of goods in transit. Goods in transit are also protected against all the other perils I've mentioned—fire, flood, tempest and so on.

SHEILA: I suppose we carry a lot of motor insurance?

GLYN: Naturally. All the company vehicles are insured through this department. As a matter of fact, I'm often asked to advise on private insurance matters by our employees.

SHEILA: When employees travel on the company's behalf, are they insured?

GLYN: Naturally—and so are their belongings. Our Travellers and Baggage insurances are arranged on a declaration basis.

SHEILA: What does that mean?

GLYN: We keep a record of all journeys made by our employees and declare them at the end of each calendar month. The insurance company charges us a premium based on the number of journeys made and the number of days the travellers are away from home. As a matter of fact, you'll know more about that when you've done that tape—the monthly declaration figures are on it!

SHEILA: Well, thank you, Mr Glyn. That's very interesting. I'll get on with your work now.

GLYN: Thank you very much.

Lesson Notes

to stand in = to deputize
a touch of 'flu = a mild attack of influenza

That's a tall one! (coll.) = that's a difficult question.
cover = protection (insurance)
to suspend operations = to cease operations for a period

Comprehension

1. Why was Sheila asked to do some work for Mr Glyn?
2. What was the matter with Mr Glyn's secretary?
3. What kind of work did Mr Glyn give Sheila?
4. What do you understand by *perils*, from the point of view of insurance?
5. What is meant by consequential loss?
6. What is meant by *Goods in Transit*?
7. What is meant by *Public Liability*?
8. What is meant by *Employer's Liability*?
9. How are Travellers and Baggage insurances handled at Discovery Engineering?
10. What does this involve?

38 The Accounts Department

Introduction

When the company was first formed, Mr Miles—who is a Chartered Accountant—ran the Accounts Department with the help of one senior and two junior clerks. As the company expanded and the work of the department increased, more staff were recruited and the department was broken down into sections. Further expansion made the appointment of another qualified accountant necessary; mechanized accounting systems were adopted and the functions of the department were separated into two main categories: Financial Accounting and Management Accounting. After a while, an assistant accountant was appointed to take charge of the Financial Accounting procedures and the Chief Accountant concentrated on the Management Accounts. However, the Chief Accountant still retained overall responsibility for the whole department and reported directly to the Financial Director.

Because of the confidential nature of the work, much of the typing required by the accountants was handled in Mr Miles's department instead of being passed to the typing pool. One day, Sheila was asked to type a report. As she had one or two queries, she went to see the assistant accountant, Bob Drew.

Dialogue

SHEILA: Sorry to bother you, Bob, but I can't quite understand this.
BOB: What's up—can't you read my writing?
SHEILA: What does this say?
BOB: Let's have a look—oh yes, that's *Fixed Assets* and *Current Assets*.
SHEILA: What's the difference?
BOB: *Fixed Assets* include things like land and buildings, plant and machinery, vehicles and so on. *Current Assets* are raw materials, work in progress, stocks of finished goods, cash in hand and at the bank and sundry debtors.
SHEILA: *Sundry debtors?*
BOB: Various people who owe us money.
SHEILA: What about *current liabilities*—I suppose they represent money owed by the company?
BOB: That's right—items such as corporation tax, dividends and trade creditors.

SHEILA: This report refers to *financial accounting* and *management accounting*. What's the difference?

BOB: *Financial accounting* is concerned with recording the day-to-day income and expenditure of the company—sales and purchases, wages and salaries, petty cash and expenses and so on. It also deals with National Insurance, PAYE, VAT and credit control.

SHEILA: What's *credit control*?

BOB: A system for making sure that we don't allow customers to have too much credit.

SHEILA: How does that operate?

BOB: We normally supply customers on a net monthly account basis; that is, they pay each month for goods supplied the previous month. When we open a new account we take up references and set a credit limit.

SHEILA: And the credit control system ensures that the monthly limit isn't exceeded?

BOB: That's the idea. Of course, credit limits are often raised, once a customer has established goodwill by settling his account regularly.

SHEILA: What happens with customers who don't pay up on the due date?

BOB: First, we send a statement showing the amount which is overdue. If the customer doesn't pay, we send a reminder with a red sticker on it; that often does the trick. After that, we have a series of letters ranging from *You appear to have overlooked this item* or *We should appreciate early settlement* to *Unless your cheque is received within seven days we shall have no alternative* ... etcetera.

SHEILA: And if he still doesn't pay?

BOB: If it's a small amount we write it off as a bad debt. For larger sums we take legal steps to recover the money. Your department looks after that.

SHEILA: What about *management accounting*? What does that consist of?

BOB: It's concerned with supplying information to management, to enable them to plan their objectives and control their budgets. It helps them to measure the profitability of products, establish break-even points and so on. It also operates cost control systems over the various sections.

SHEILA: To make sure they keep within their budgets?

BOB: Not so much that as to check on their cost-effectiveness. Take R & D, for example. If they spend too much money developing a product, we may lose money on it even if it sells well.

SHEILA: When I first came here, people were talking about things like *break-even points* and *cost-effectiveness*. I didn't know then what they were talking about, but I'm beginning to understand.

Lesson Notes

broken down into sections = divided into sections
Sorry to bother you, but ... This is an informal way of apologizing for interrupting or disturbing someone. Some more formal ways of doing this are: *Please excuse this interruption, but ... I'm sorry to intrude, but ... I hope I'm not disturbing you, but ... Forgive me for interrupting/disturbing you, but ...*
What's up? (coll.) = What's the matter?
goodwill = an atmosphere or state of trust which results from regular, satisfactory trading.
to pay up *(coll.)* = to settle one's account
That often does the trick (coll.) = that often has the desired effect.

Comprehension

1   What qualification has Mr Miles got?
2   What did the Accounts Department consist of when the company was first formed?
3   What changes were brought about by the expansion of the company?
4   What two main categories of accounting are carried out by the department?
5   Who is the Chief Accountant responsible to?
6   Why is much of the accountants' typing handled in Mr Miles's department?
7   What is the difference between Fixed and Current Assets?
8   What is the difference between assets and liabilities?
9   What is financial accounting?
10 What is management accounting?
11 What is the purpose of a credit control system?
12 How are *slow payers* encouraged to settle their accounts?
13 What is a bad debt?
14 What is the purpose of a cost control system?

39 A Trip Abroad

Introduction

While Sheila was learning about the functions of the Secretarial and Accounts Departments, David was working in the Overseas Department. One of his first assignments was to make a translation of the brochure currently being prepared by the Advertising Section for CP21. Now that it had definitely been decided to go ahead with the product, there was a great deal of work to be done in all departments.

Because of design modifications necessitated by the combination of CP21 and SPOT, some alterations to the production drawings and machine tool designs were necessary, and both Global and Discovery wanted to subject the product to further tests. It was agreed that these should take place in the Global works and that Bill Pound, the Manufacturing Director, should attend. Since not all the Global engineers spoke English it was decided to take an interpreter, and David was asked to go. He was naturally very excited at the prospect and was anxious to tell Sheila as soon as possible. He asked her to have lunch with him at the Castle Hotel restaurant.

Dialogue

SHEILA: Whatever's all the excitement about? And what's wrong with the canteen? This is much too expensive!
DAVID: To-day we're celebrating!
SHEILA: Celebrating what? Is it your birthday?
DAVID: Much more exciting than that. I'm having a trip abroad with Mr Pound. He's going to visit the Global Engineering factory and he needs an interpreter.
SHEILA: How thrilling! When do you leave?
DAVID: In a few days' time. They haven't fixed the exact date—there's still quite a lot to do before they're ready to run these tests.
SHEILA: How long will you be away?
DAVID: It depends on how well things go. Two or three days at the most, I'd say.
SHEILA: Well, congratulations! How will you travel?
DAVID: By plane from Heathrow, I suppose. I don't know any details yet.
SHEILA: There's a direct air link between Birmingham and Heathrow, isn't there?

DAVID: Yes, I believe there is. But I have a feeling that most of our people prefer to go to London by train.
SHEILA: By Inter-City to Euston, you mean?
DAVID: That's right. Sometimes they travel up to London the evening before and spend the night at a hotel near the airport.
SHEILA: I shouldn't think you'd get much sleep—airports are pretty noisy places!
DAVID: Oh, it's not as bad as that. The windows are double-glazed and all the rooms are air-conditioned, and this cuts down the noise. Anyway, I believe there are restrictions on taking-off and landing at certain times during the night.
SHEILA: Well, it's a great chance for you. I'm quite envious.
DAVID: It's a shame you can't come as well.
SHEILA: I don't think there's much chance of that. Still, I'm doing my bit towards getting CP21 off the ground.
DAVID: Oh, what's that?
SHEILA: Preparing the licensing agreement. It's a very long, involved document. We keep having to re-draft clauses and send them off to our solicitor for approval.
DAVID: When will the agreement be signed?
SHEILA: Not yet awhile. But I don't suppose production will be delayed because the actual documents aren't ready. After all, everything's been agreed in principle and we've already exchanged drawings and specifications with Global.
DAVID: I wonder what they're going to call the product. I need to know that soon for my brochure.
SHEILA: They ought to combine the names, just as they did the designs. What about SPOT-21?
DAVID: SPOT-21 eh? That has quite a ring to it! Why don't you suggest it? You might get an award under the suggestions scheme!
SHEILA: Maybe I will. If I win, I'll stand you a lunch!
DAVID: I'll hold you to that!
SHEILA: Heavens, look at the time! I must fly—some of us have to work, you know!

Lesson Notes

to run (a test)=to carry out
I'm doing my bit (coll.)=I'm making a contribution, playing a useful part.
We keep having to re-draft clauses=it is frequently necessary for us to re-draft clauses.
clauses=paragraph (of an agreement)
not yet awhile=not for some time yet
That has quite a ring to it!=that sounds quite impressive.

I'll stand you a lunch! (coll.) = I'll invite you to lunch.
I'll hold you to that! (coll.) = I'll make sure that you keep that promise.
I must fly! (coll.) = I must hurry away.

Comprehension

1 What was one of David's first assignments in the Overseas Department?
2 Why was it necessary to change the production drawings?
3 What other changes had to be made?
4 Where were the additional tests to be carried out?
5 Why was David asked to accompany the Manufacturing Director to the Global works?
6 Why did David invite Sheila to lunch at the Castle Hotel restaurant?
7 How long did David expect to be away?
8 How did he expect to travel?
9 How are airport hotels protected against the noise from aircraft?
10 What part was Sheila playing in the launching of the new product?
11 Why was the preparation of the document taking such a long time?
12 Was this going to delay production?
13 Why did David think Sheila should suggest the name SPOT-21 to the management?
14 What promise did Sheila make to David?

40 Spot-21 Is Launched

Introduction

From being a little-known, highly specialized device designed to solve one customer's particular problem, CP21 has been developed into a major product to which the Production, Marketing and Overseas Departments of both Discovery Engineering and Global Engineering have given a great deal of attention. The combined resources of the two companies have been concentrated on a joint sales promotion campaign which is to culminate in a special display at a London trade exhibition early in the New Year. Less than three months after the opening of negotiations between Discovery and Global, SPOT-21 is to be launched.

Mr Blake and an engineer from R & D have visited each of the regional offices in turn to brief the sales representatives on the new product. The Advertising Section has prepared a series of advertisements, press releases and other publicity material to coincide with the official launching. Meanwhile, the final tests in the Global factory have been successfully carried out and the results analysed by computer. Everyone is optimistic about the prospects for SPOT-21.

Of the several hundred employees of Discovery Engineering, three are especially interested in SPOT-21. These are John Edwards, the Product Manager, and Sheila Smith and David Long, who joined the company just as the original product—formerly known as CP21—was being developed. The day before the official launch, these three arrange to meet for a celebration lunch at the Castle Hotel restaurant.

Dialogue

DAVID: Here's the menu, John. Take your pick—it's Sheila's treat!
SHEILA: Hey, who says so?
DAVID: Don't you remember? You said that if they adopted your idea of calling the new product SPOT-21 ...!
SHEILA: Oh yes—well, I've got news for you! About a dozen other people had the same idea!
JOHN: So you didn't get an award after all?
SHEILA: Afraid not—but as it's my birthday, I'll buy the plonk.
JOHN: What a nice girl! Now, what shall we have? Sheila, what are you going to start with?

SHEILA: Some soup, I think—and then a steak with a green salad.
WAITER: How do you like your steak, madam?
SHEILA: Medium rare, please.
DAVID: I'll have a steak too—rare, please. And some French fried potatoes and peas.
WAITER: Anything to start with, sir?
DAVID: Yes—a grapefruit cocktail, please.
JOHN: I'll have a prawn cocktail to start with, and Chicken Maryland to follow.
WAITER: What vegetables would you like with the chicken, sir?
JOHN: Some French fries and green beans, please.
WAITER: Very good, sir. Would you like anything to drink?
JOHN: Yes, bring the wine list, please ... thank you. Now, what's it to be?
DAVID: What goes well with steak and chicken?
SHEILA: How about a rosé?
JOHN: Is that OK for you, David?
DAVID: Yes, fine.
JOHN: All right. One bottle of No. 15, please.
WAITER: Thank you, sir.
DAVID: D'you realize we have another anniversary to celebrate?
JOHN: No—what's that?
SHEILA: David and I have both been at Discovery for exactly one year!
JOHN: Well, fancy that! Have they said anything about permanent assignments yet?
DAVID: Not exactly, but I've hinted strongly that I'd like to stay in the Overseas Department if possible. I think there's an opening there for me but it's not been officially confirmed yet.
SHEILA: And I'd like to stay in Stephen's department if it can be arranged. Marion Clark's having a baby so she'll be leaving in a few months.
JOHN: Oh—it's 'Stephen' already, is it? However did you manage to get so familiar with our august Mr Miles?
SHEILA: I know he seems a bit forbidding at times, but he's very nice when you get to know him.
DAVID: So it would appear!
JOHN: Here's our wine. Let's drink to the success of SPOT-21.
ALL: SPOT-21!

Lesson Notes

Take your pick—it's Sheila's treat! (*coll.*) = Choose what you want—Sheila is paying for everyone.
plonk (*coll.*) = wine
What a nice girl! What a ...! or *What ...!* is an idiomatic form often used to draw attention to the particular qualities of a person or thing. It is often used, for example, when commenting on the weather: *What a lovely day! What dreadful weather we're having!*
medium rare: a steak cooked *medium rare* is brown on the outside and pink inside; one cooked *rare* is brown outside but red inside. A *well done* steak is cooked until it is brown right through.
... our august Mr Miles: Mr Miles evidently has a reputation for being rather superior and unapproachable.

Comprehension

1. How is SPOT-21 going to be launched?
2. What product training has been given to the sales representatives?
3. What part has the Advertising Department played in the launching of SPOT-21?
4. How were the test results analyzed?
5. Which three employees of Discovery Engineering are particularly interested in SPOT-21?
6. How do they celebrate the launching?
7. Why does Sheila offer to buy the wine?
8. Why didn't Sheila get an award for naming the product?
9. What else are Sheila and David celebrating?
10. What are David's hopes for the future?
11. What would Sheila like to do, if it can be arranged?
12. Why does she think this will be a possibility?

Management English—Grammar

The purpose of these notes is to provide a source of easy reference for students wishing to verify points of grammar as they arise in the Episodes. Some detailed explanations are given of points which experience has shown cause confusion to foreign students of English. The notes are, however, far from comprehensive and are not intended to replace a text-book of grammar.

1 Simple present tense of verbs, with short forms where used

   a) *be*: I am   I'm   b) *have*: I have   I've
            You are   You're*   You have   You've*
            He is   He's   He has   He's
            She is   She's   She has   She's
            It is   It's   It has   It's
            We are   We're   We have   We've
            They are   They're   They have   They've

   c) *do*: I do   d) *go*: I go
            You do*   You go*
            He does   He goes
            She does   She goes
            It does   It goes
            We do   We go
            They do   They go

   e) All regular verbs, and most irregular verbs in the present tense:

       Model verb: *listen*   I listen
                                  You listen*
                                  He listens
                                  She listens
                                  It listens
                                  We listen
                                  They listen

   *the *you* form is the same in both singular and plural.

2 Present continuous tense of all verbs including *be* (except certain defective verbs). This tense is formed with the present simple of *be* + the present participle (the *-ing* form) of the main verb:

I am	being	doing	having	going	listening
You are	,,	,,	,,	,,	,,
He is	,,	,,	,,	,,	,,
She is	,,	,,	,,	,,	,,
It is	,,	,,	,,	,,	,,
We are	,,	,,	,,	,,	,,
They are	,,	,,	,,	,,	,,

Note: in this tense, and in ALL continuous tenses, only the auxiliary changes its form. The present participle is invariable.

3 Imperative Mood

The second persons singular and plural are the same as the infinitive:
 (You) Listen!   Listen to me!
The first person plural is formed thus:
 Let us (let's) + infinitive: Let's listen! Let's listen to the radio.

4 Formation of Questions

a) When the main verb is *be*, questions are formed by inversion of subject and verb:
 I am (I'm) a student.   Am I a student?
 He is (he's) the manager.   Is he the manager?

b) In compound tenses, the subject and auxiliary are inverted:
 They are (they're) listening.   Are they listening?

c) When the main verb is *have*, questions may be formed in two ways:

 i) by inversion of subject and verb: They have a car. Have they a car?
 ii) by using *do* as an auxiliary (see note (d) below):
   They have a car.   Do they have a car?
   He has a car.   Does he have a car?
 Note: Many people say *have got* instead of *have*—the meaning is the same.
 Questions are formed by inversion of subject and main verb; *got* is invariable.
   They have (they've) got a car.   Have they got a car?
   He has (he's) got a car.   Has he got a car?

d) All other verbs (except defective verbs which are dealt with later) form questions by using *do* as an auxiliary:

I listen to the radio.   Do I listen to the radio?
He listens to the   Does he listen to the teacher?
teacher.
Only the auxiliary changes its form. The main verb is in the infinitive and is invariable.

e) When questions begin with: What? Who? Where? or How? and any part of the verb *be* as the *main* verb, the construction is:

question word	+ verb	+ subject
What	is	Discovery Engineering Ltd?
Who	is	Mr Green?
Where	are	the sales offices?
How old	is	David?

In continuous tenses the construction is:

question word	+ auxiliary	+ subject	+ present participle (-*ing*)
What	is	David	doing?
Where	are	the trainees	going?

f) When questions are introduced by question words with part of *have* or *have got* as the main verb, the construction may vary thus:
  i) What have you in your hand?
  ii) What do you have in your hand?
  iii) What have you got in your hand? (This is the most usual in everyday speech in England.)

g) When questions are introduced by question words with a main verb other than *be* or *have*, the auxiliary *do* is again used:
  Where does Mr Green work?
  Where do David and Sheila work?
  What does Mr Green do for a living?
  Who do you work for?

5   The personal pronouns and possessive adjectives

I	my	It	its
You	your	We	our
He	his	They	their
She	her		

6   *be* + *going to* + infinitive of a verb implies a future action already planned or decided: Mr Green *is going to tell* David about his job.
Do not confuse this with the present continuous tense of *go*: David *is going* to Mr Green's office.

7 Prepositions *in* and *into*

in implies position: The factory is in Birmingham
into implies movement: David goes into the office
in may occasionally be used to express motion: He put the book in (or into) his briefcase.
But *into* can NEVER express position. We CANNOT say: *He is into the office*. *into* must always have an expressed object; after *in* the object may be omitted. Thus we say: *Come into my office! Come in!*

8 Formation of negatives

a) with *be* as the main verb, the negative is formed by placing *not* after the verb:
He is (he's) a director. He is not (isn't) a director.
The full negative form of the present tense of *be*, with short forms, is as follows:

I am not	I'm not	
You are not	You're not	or You aren't
He is not	He's not	,, He isn't
She is not	She's not	,, She isn't
It is not	It's not	,, It isn't
We are not	We're not	,, We aren't
They are not	They're not	,, They aren't

Either of the short forms may be used. The first is slightly more emphatic:
I'm going to borrow your car. Oh no you're NOT!

b) In continuous tenses, *not* is placed between auxiliary and participle:
We are (we're) listening. We are not (we're not, we aren't) listening.

c) When *have* is the main verb, the negative may be formed either:
i) by placing *not* after the verb, in which case the short form is normally used:
I have a car.   I haven't a car.
He has a car.   He hasn't a car.

or ii) by using *do* as auxiliary:
I have a car.   I do not (don't) have a car.
He has a car.   He does not (doesn't) have a car.

d) When *have got* is the main verb, *not* is placed between *have* and *got*:
I have (I've) got a car.   I have not (haven't) got a car.
He has (he's) got a car   He has not (hasn't) got a car

e) With simple tenses of all other verbs (except defective verbs) we use *do* + *not* thus:
I do not (don't) listen.   He does not (doesn't) listen.

f) The negative of the imperative is formed thus:
Listen!   Do not (don't) listen!
Let's listen!   Let's not listen!   Do not (don't) let's listen!

g) Negative questions. There are two possible word orders, one using the short form and the other the full form of *not*. The short form is the more usual:
He isn't at work to-day.   Isn't he at work to-day?
He doesn't work in Advertising.   Doesn't he work in Advertising?

but the full form is sometimes used:
He is not at work.   Is he not at work?
He does not work here.   Does he not work here?

9 Possessive forms

Nouns in the singular add *'s*: Mr Green's office. The manager's car.
Plural nouns ending in *s* add *'* only: The managers' cars.
Plural nouns *not* ending in *s* add *'s*: The men's cloakroom.
Some proper names ending in *s* take *'s* to form the possessive:
    St James's Park.   Mr Jones's car.
The possessive of inanimate objects is more usually formed with *of*, thus:
    The roof of the house.   (not 'the house's roof')
We sometimes use this construction when speaking of people:
    The home of Mr and Mrs Jones.

10 Object forms of the personal pronouns (direct and indirect)

me	(I)	it	(it)
you	(you)	us	(we)
him	(he)	them	(they)
her	(she)		

11 The impersonal pronouns *one* and *ones*

These are often used in conversation to avoid repetition:
Is there a staff canteen?   Yes, it's a very good one.
Bring me the brochures.   Which ones do you want?
The ones on my desk.

12 Emphatic and reflexive pronouns

Myself   (I)
Yourself (pl. Yourselves)   (you)
Himself   (he)
Herself   (she)
Itself   (it)
Ourselves   (we)
Themselves   (they)

Note also the impersonal form *oneself* corresponding to *one* in such constructions as: One cannot do everything by oneself.
Students should be careful when using this type of construction, as in certain contexts it may sound formal.
These forms are reflexive in function when the subject and object are the same: I'm here to make myself useful. She cut herself with a knife.
When they are emphatic in function they can serve to emphasize either the subject or the object, depending on the construction:
I gave it to the manager *myself* = I personally gave it to the manager
I gave it to the manager *himself* = I gave it to the manager, and not to some other person acting for him.

13 The demonstrative adjectives and pronouns: *this that these those*

This and its plural *these* indicate things which are close to the speaker, either literally or in time. *That* and *those* indicate things comparatively distant.
I'll buy this book (in my hand). I don't want those (over there).
Is that your case over there? No, this is my case (here beside me).
In those days (last century) there was no electricity.
Everything is very expensive these days.

14 Order and position of adjectives

The normal position of an adjective is before the noun:
A pretty girl.   A naughty child.
Adjectives may be used predicatively:
That girl is pretty.   The child is naughty.
When there is more than one adjective, the most specific is placed immediately before the noun:
A young university student.   An old Roman coin.
When the adjectives are of equal value—that is, purely descriptive—the shorter is usually placed first:
A smart, attractive woman.   A good, economical car.
and the adjectives separated by commas.

15 The defective verb *can* (infinitive: *be able*)

The only forms of this verb are the simple present and the simple past:
I, you, he, she, it, we, they can/could (*Note:* The conditional is also *could*)
The negative forms are: *cannot* (*can't*) and *could not* (*couldn't*)
Questions are formed by inversion of subject and verb: Can I help you?
can is always followed by a second verb, either expressed or understood, which is in the infinitive.
All other tenses are taken from the infinitive *be able*.
Note: be able requires the preposition *to* before the second verb, but *can* does not.
He can come this afternoon. *But:* He is not able to come to-morrow.

16 Future tense (all except defective verbs)

This is formed with the auxiliaries *shall* or *will* + the infinitive of the main verb:
I shall listen
You will   ,,
He will   ,,
She will   ,,
It will   ,,
We shall   ,,
They will ,,

The negative is formed by placing *not* after the auxiliary:
I shall not (shan't) listen
They will not (won't) listen
and the interrogative by inverting subject and auxiliary:
Shall we listen?
Will he listen?
Where it is intended to express determination, willingness,

intention or wish, the use of the auxiliaries *shall* and *will* is reversed:
I will listen = I want, intend, am willing to listen
You shall listen = I want, intend, am willing for you to listen
The short form -'*ll* replaces both *shall* and *will*, and in spoken, everyday English the distinction is frequently ignored.

17 Use of *will* to imply habit, tendency, refusal to do or to stop doing something:
He will not (won't) tell me where he is going = He refuses to tell me.
The children will keep interrupting (despite being told to be quiet).
She will gossip and spread rumours (she persists in doing this).
There is no futurity in this use of *will*. The word is normally given additional stress when used in conversation.

18 Questions beginning with *how*
   a) When *how* is followed by an adverb or adjective, the question calls for a reply which is relevant to that adverb or adjective:

How large is your house?	It has ten rooms.
How fast is your car?	It can do 100 miles an hour.
How far is it to Birmingham?	It's about ten miles.

   b) When *how* is immediately followed by a verb and its subject, the meaning is the same as *in what manner?* and the reply should be worded accordingly.

   | How is Ruth dressed? | She's wearing a blue skirt and a white blouse. |

19 Questions beginning with *what where who* and *how* followed by a verb needing *do* as auxiliary for the formation of questions.
Here the construction is as follows:

Question word +	auxiliary +	subject +	main verb	(+ predicate)
What	does	Ruth	look	like?
Where	does	Ruth	take	Sheila and David?
Who*	do	Sheila and David	meet?	
How	does	this machine	work?	

In compound tenses, when using defective verbs such as *can* which are followed by a second verb, and with *have got*, the construction is:

What	shall	we	do	this evening?
Where	can	I	find	Mr Green?
Who*	will	they	send	to London?
What	have	you	got	in your case?

See also note 4(e)

*In this construction, *who* is in the accusative case and should strictly speaking become *whom*. However, in everyday speech *whom* is seldom heard except in such constructions as *The man to whom I was speaking*; even this is more usually rendered as *The man I was speaking to*.

20 Questions beginning with *why*

The word order is the same as that for direct questions (see Note 4 a), b), c), d) and negative questions (see Note 8 g)):

Do you listen to the radio?	Why do you listen to the radio?
Is he the manager?	Why is he the manager?
Are you learning English?	Why are you learning English?
Isn't he at work to-day?	Why isn't he at work to-day?
Doesn't he work in Advertising?	Why doesn't he work in Advertising?

21 *How, what, where, who,* and *why* as conjunctions

There is no inversion of subject and verb after these words when they are used as conjunctions, even when they introduce an indirect question:

Mrs Wood explains how the section is organized.
David asks Mrs Wood how the section is organized.

Mrs Wood tells David what he has to do.
David asks Mrs Wood what he has to do.

Ruth shows Sheila where the canteen is.
Sheila asks Ruth where the canteen is.

Mr Green tells Sheila who is in charge of marketing.
Sheila asks Mr Green who is in charge of marketing.

Mrs Wood tells David why printing blocks are expensive.
David asks Mrs Wood why printing blocks are expensive.

22　*some* and *any*

some is generally used in affirmative sentences and *any* in negative and interrogative sentences.

I'll have some coffee, please.	I don't want any coffee, thank you.
Have you any cigarettes?	Yes, there are some on the table.
Here's some coffee; do you want any?	No thank you, I've got some.

However, when offering something to a person, *some* is often used interrogatively: Would you like some coffee? Do you want some sugar?

23　*Something* and *anything*

These are used in a similar way to *some* and *any*.
I know something about advertising.
Do you know anything about advertising?
I don't know anything about advertising.

24　Relative pronoun *what*

This is used when there is no antecedent.
Tell me *what* you want to know = Tell me *the thing(s) that* you want to know.
I don't suppose that's quite what you mean = I don't suppose that's quite *the thing that* you mean.

25　Formation of adverbs

Many adverbs are formed by adding *-ly* to an adjective:
rare, rarely　safe, safely　tight, tightly
Some adjectives ending in *-y* change this to *i-* before adding *ly*:
happy, happily　merry, merrily
Note the irregular forms:
good (adj)　well (adv)
fast　(adj)　fast (adv)
far　(adj)　far (adv)

26　*have to* + infinitive

This indicates necessity or compulsion:
You have to pass a test before you can drive a car.
We have to leave now to catch our train.

The auxiliary *do* is normally used for both negative and interrogative forms:
   You don't have to come if you don't want to.
   Do I have to fill in this form?
Have got to conveys the same idea of necessity, but is normally only used when speaking of a particular case.
Compare: I have to telephone the printers (as part of my normal duties, every day etc.)
with: I've got to telephone the printers (because the proofs are overdue)

27 The passive voice

This is very commonly used in English. It is formed with the verb *be* and the past participle of the main verb.
Compare: A very wide range of industries use our products (active)
with: Our products are used by a very wide range of industries (passive)
The agent, or *doer* of the action expressed in the verb is not always stated:
   Mrs Wood explains how they organize the section (active)
   Mrs Wood explains how the section is organized (by them) (passive)
Note the infinitive construction:
   We have to make special blocks (active)
   Special blocks have to be made (passive)
and the continuous tense:
   The man is driving the car (active)
   The car is being driven by the man (passive)
IN ALL USES OF THE PASSIVE VOICE, THE VERB *BE* IS IN THE SAME TENSE OR FORM AS THE MAIN VERB WOULD BE IN THE CORRESPONDING ACTIVE CONSTRUCTION.

28 Prepositions *to* and *at*

to implies movement towards: David goes down to the ground floor.
at implies position: They meet at the entrance to the canteen.

29 Past participle of regular verbs

This is normally formed by the addition of *-d* for verbs ending in *-e*:
   estimate, estimated   bake, baked
Verbs ending in *-p*, *-d* or *-t* double the final letter before adding *-ed*:
   stop, stopped   prod, prodded   pat, patted

171

Verbs ending in -*y* after a consonant change this to *i*- before adding -*ed*:
 marry, married   try, tried
Other regular verbs add -*ed*:   listen, listened   employ, employed

30 Formation of present perfect tense (all except defective verbs)

This tense is formed with the present tense of *have* and the past participle of the main verb:
 I have been   He has been
 They have had   He has had
 He has gone   We have done
 She has listened You have tried   etc.
The participle is invariable.
(*Note:* No attempt is made here to deal with irregular verbs, since these are only irregular in the formation of their past participle and simple past. Otherwise, they behave exactly like regular verbs.)

31 Use of present perfect tense

This tense is often used when speaking of an action, begun and completed in the past, which still has some effect on or connection with the present:
 I have (I've) telephoned the printers and they say the proofs are ready.
It is also used when speaking of an indefinite time in the past:
 I've been to France many times.

32 Formation of present perfect continuous tense

This tense is formed with the present perfect of *be* and the present participle of the main verb:
 I have been (I've been) listening. He has been (he's been) listening.
The participle is invariable.

33 Use of the present perfect continuous tense

This tense is used to express an action which began in the past, continued over a period and is possibly still going on:
 I've been working very hard this morning.
 I've been living in this house for ten years.

34 Present participle/verbal noun (the -*ing* form)

The present participle is often used in English to describe an action in progress at the same time as that of the main verb:

I spent this morning *chasing* proofs and *studying* literature
He sits in his chair all the evening *watching* television
The verbal noun (gerund) has the same form:
Advertising is an important part of selling

35 *a little a few much many a lot of*

a little and *much* are used with singular uncountable nouns to indicate an indefinite quantity:
A little mint sauce, please.   Not too much milk, thank you.
A few and *many* are used with plural countable nouns to indicate an indefinite number:
Just a few beans, please.   Many people take sugar in coffee.
A lot of can be used before either singular or plural nouns, and is normally preferred to *much* in an affirmative sense in spoken English.
I like a lot of sugar in my tea (preferable to: I like much sugar . . .)
A lot of people drink black coffee=many people drink black coffee

36 *Must/must not (mustn't)* with infinitive of main verb

This defective verb indicates necessity or obligation (must) and prohibition (must not).
You must study this lesson (because it is necessary)
You must not discuss that (because it is forbidden)
The passive construction is very common:
It must be done at once
He must not be told about the new product
Questions are formed by inversion:
Must you go now?
Must I fill in this form?
must is also used to express strong probability:
You must be tired after your long journey
must exists only in the present tense; all other tenses are expressed by *have to* or *have got to* (see note 26) or *need* (see note 37).

37 Need/need not (needn't)

If we wish to indicate that something is unnecessary, we use *need not* before the main verb.
You needn't fill in that form=It is not necessary for you to fill it in
We needn't do this to-day

173

Need is a regular verb; when followed by a second verb in the infinitive it has a similar function to *must*. Questions may be formed either by inversion or by using the auxiliary *do*:
   *I need to cash a travellers cheque.
   *Do I need to fill in this form?
   Need I sign the form?
When *need* is used transitively questions can only be formed using the auxiliary *do* (other than in compound tenses):
   Do I need a visa?   Shall I need my umbrella?
*Note that these constructions require *to* before the infinitive.

38   Comparative form of adjectives and adverbs

Regular short adjectives are compared by adding *-er* (or *-r* where the word ends in *-e*)
   safe, safer   cheap, cheaper   loud, louder
Adjectives ending in *-y* preceded by a consonant change *-y* to *i-* before adding *-er*:
   happy, happier   silly, sillier
Note the irregular: good, better   bad, worse
Longer adjectives are compared by placing *more* in front:
   expensive, more expensive   difficult, more difficult
Adverbs of two or more syllables form their comparatives by placing *more* in front: more quickly   more expensively
Adverbs of one syllable (and the adverb *early*) add-*er*:
   fast, faster   early, earlier   high, higher
The superlative form is used when comparing three or more items. adjectives and adverbs which form their comparatives with *-er* add *-est* for the superlative:
Adj: safe, safer safest   Adv: fast, faster, fastest
   cheap, cheaper, cheapest   early, earlier, earliest
Adjectives and adverbs which are compared with *more* form their superlatives with *most*:
   expensive, more expensive, most expensive
   expensively, more expensively, most expensively

39   Passive voice—future tense

As with all other passive forms, the tense is expressed by the appropriate form of *be*:
   The brochure will be modified
   We shall be told about the product at the meeting

40   *Should* expressing obligation

In addition to its function as the past and conditional forms of *shall* (see note 52), *should* is used to express a duty,

obligation or desirable state of affairs.
It is sometimes qualified by *really*:
You really should visit your mother (because it is your duty)
We really should include the technical data (it is preferable)
Should I fill in this form? (is it necessary?)

should can also express probability:
If you start in good time, you should catch the train easily.

The negative is *should not* (*shouldn't*).

41 Passive voice—present perfect tense

These same rule applies as in note 39; the tense is expressed by *be* and the past participle of the main verb is invariable:
The amendments have been made.
The literature has been up-dated.

42 *so* replacing a phrase or sentence

so is frequently used in this way in conversation, to avoid repetition.
Is Mr Green a director? I think so. (=I think he is a director)
I know he likes his job, because he says so. (=he says he likes his job)
Is Sheila in the office? I don't think so.

so may also be used to indicate that a second person, thing, place etc. has something in common with the first; again, this is to avoid repetition.
Mrs Wood is in advertising. So is David. (=David is also in advertising)
Ruth is a secretary. So is Mary.
Sheila works for Discovery Engineering. So does Mrs Wood

Note: after a negative statement, we use *neither* as follows:
Mrs Wood isn't in Marketing. Neither is David.
Ruth doesn't work for Mrs Wood. Neither do I.

43 *the former* and *the latter*

These are used to distinguish between two things or people previously mentioned. Where three or more things or people are mentioned, *first*, *second* etc. and *last* are used. We sometimes say *the first-named*, *the last-mentioned* etc. An example of this is given in note 40.

44   The future continuous tense

This is formed with the future of *be* and the present participle of the main verb:
   We shall be listening   They will be listening
This tense is often used to express a planned future action, or anticipated state of affairs, and is frequently interchangeable with the simple future, the present continuous or the *going to* form. Thus:
   Mr Green will come to see you this afternoon
   Mr Green is coming to see you this afternoon
   Mr Green is going to come to see you this afternoon
   Mr Green will be coming to see you this afternoon
all express the same idea.

45   The emphatic *do*

a) Used with the imperative, it gives added force and at the same time adds a friendly or persuasive note to a polite command:
   Do come in! (more welcoming than simply: Come in!)
   Do let me know if you need any help. (emphasizing the speaker's willingness to help)

b) in affirmative constructions in the indicative mood, *do* and *does* give additional emphasis to the main verb:
   I do like your house!

c) In short answers, *do* avoids repetition of the main verb or the entire predicate.
   Do you like your   Yes, I do (like my work)
   work?
   Do you smoke?   No, I don't (smoke)
   Does David smoke?   Yes, he does.

d) In comparative constructions, *do* is frequently used to avoid repetition:
   He drives a car better than I do (=better than I drive a car)
   I work harder than he does (=harder than he works)

46   The simple past tense

This is used to refer to events wholly past and having no obvious link with or effect on the present:
   We went to France last year.   They arrived home late last night.
For those verbs which need the auxiliary *do* to form questions and negative statements (see notes 4 and 8), the tense is indicated by the auxiliary, the main verb being in the infinitive.

Where did you go for your holidays? We went to France.
They didn't go to the theatre; they went to a concert.
Note: Even for a very recent event, the simple past is used if the time when it took place is specified.
Compare: I spoke to the printers a few minutes ago.
with: I've spoken to the printers.
The former example confines the event to a specified time; the latter does not.

47 The question tag

English conversation is full of statements which end with short questions such as *isn't it?, shall we?, don't they?* These cause much confusion to foreign students of the language. Question tags are added to statements which the speaker wishes to be confirmed or agreed to by the person to whom he is speaking. Most languages have an invariable phrase for this purpose; for example: *n'est-ce pas? verdad? nicht wahr? non e vero?* In English, the form of the question tag depends on the original statement. There are two basic rules.
i) an affirmative statement is followed by a negative question tag, and vice versa.
ii) The question tag is formed by inverting the subject and verb (or subject and auxiliary if a compound tense is used) before changing affirmative to negative or negative to affirmative.

There's (there is) some pretty country round here, isn't there? (is there not?)
There are some pretty villages near here, aren't there? (are there not?)
You don't (do not) come from Birmingham, do you?
That claim is a bit far-fetched, isn't it? (is it not?)

Note that a pronoun is always used in the question tag even when the original subject is named.
Here are some further examples of sentences ending with question tags:

Mr and Mrs Brown don't live in London, do they?
David comes from Surrey, doesn't he? (does he not?)
Mr Green is a director, isn't he? (is he not?)
You're studying English, aren't you? (are you not?)

Note the irregular form *aren't I?*: I'm late, aren't I? (am I not?) An understanding of the basic rules and examples given above will help the student to grasp the meaning of question tags when they are used by English speakers, and eventually to use them actively if desired.

48 *had better* (invariable) with infinitive of main verb

This idiom indicates that an action is advisable (affirmative) or inadvisable (negative). *Had* is frequently shortened to *'d* in spoken English.
   You'd better write that again.
   You'd better leave now to catch the train.
   You'd better not be late for your appointment.
When used to a subordinate, it is equivalent to an instruction.

49 *ago* in expressions of time

ago following a word or phrase expressing a space of time, indicates the length of time between the moment of speaking and a previous event. The event may be stated either before or after the *ago* phrase:
   I came to this town six years ago.
   Three years ago, the company extended its factory.
   I last saw him several years ago.

50 Defective verb *may* (past tense: *might*)
This verb is always followed by a second verb, either expressed or implied.
It has two main uses:
i) to request or grant permission: May I call you Sheila? May I smoke? Yes, you may.
ii) to express possibility: I may go abroad this year.

Note: In examples such as those given in (i), *may* is often replaced by *can*. It is not strictly correct, but is widely accepted in everyday speech.

51 Possessive before a gerund (the *-ing* form of a verb)

   You don't mind my calling you Sheila, do you?
This rule is frequently ignored in everyday speech; many people would say:
   You don't mind me calling you Sheila, do you?

52 Conditional sentences

The conditional forms of the auxiliary and defective verbs *shall will can* and *may* are the same as their past tense:
   Shall → should
   Will → would
   May → might
   Can → could

Most conditional sentences are formed in one of two ways:
i) present+future: If we go ahead, we'll (=we shall) need more workers.
ii) past+conditional: If they went ahead, they'd (they would) need more workers.
i) is used when speaking of a strong probability; (ii) is used in cases of mere possibility or when giving a hypothetical example.*
Note: There is a third form of conditional construction which deals with an impossibility (the *unfulfilled condition*):
iii) Past perfect+conditional perfect: If the company had gone ahead, it would have needed more workers.

*Some uses of these forms are illustrated in Episodes 13 and 14, and later in Episode 30 onwards.

53 Reported speech

In reported speech, every tense used in the direct speech is changed to the equivalent past tense, as follows:

Simple present	becomes	simple past
Present continuous	,,	past continuous
Present perfect	,,	past perfect
Present perfect continuous	,,	past perfect continuous

Example: David: I'm going to see Mr Blake.
This speech is reported as: David said he was going to see Mr Blake.

54 *seem to be may be* etc.

Statements such as: *There are a lot of activities* or *There is a lot of work to do* may be modified by the introduction of certain verbs—for example, *seem, may, can, must*. In such cases, the verb *be* takes the infinitive form:
   There seems to be a lot of work to do.
   There may be some problems with the new designs.
   There must be a better way of solving the problem.

55 *for* and *since* in expressions of time

for precedes a word or words indicating a space of time:
   I have been living here for a year.
   David will be in Advertising for several weeks.
   I haven't seen him for a long time.
since precedes a specific or approximate date, time or event in the past which marks the beginning of the period up to the moment of speaking.

I have been living here since last May.
David has been working in Advertising since he joined the company.
I haven't seen him since 1975.

56 *so . . . as* and *as . . . as*

The former is used in negative constructions:
   I'm not so important as that!
and the latter in affirmative constructions:
   He is as tall as his elder brother.

57 Past perfect tense

This is formed with the past tense of *have* with the past participle of the main verb. It is frequently used in reported speech (see note 53).
   Mr Blake: I've asked our Regional Managers to make enquiries.
This is reported as: Mr Blake said he had asked our Regional Managers . . .

58 Past continuous tense

This is formed with the simple past of *be* and the present participle of the main verb. It is used to indicate something that was in progress at a past time which is under consideration. Sometimes it is contrasted with the simple past.
   Compare: What were you doing when he telephoned?
   with: What did you do when he telephoned?

59 *unless* and *until*

unless is equivalent to *if . . . not . . .*
   Unless it rains, I shall go = If it doesn't rain, I shall go.
   I can't come unless my car is repaired = I can't come if my car is not repaired.
until in affirmative statements marks a date, time or event at which some activity ceased (or will cease):
   We'll stay until eight o'clock.
   He was a director of the company until two years ago.
   We waited until the rain stopped.
until in negative statements marks a date, time or event which must arrive or happen before the activity begins:
   I can't go until my car is ready.
   The meeting doesn't start until two o'clock.

60 Part of verb *be* + infinitive

This conveys the idea of a future happening with some degree of intention or compulsion.

He is to work in advertising.
I am to tell you that Mr Green is coming to see you.
The new product is to be launched at the sales convention.*

*Note that this example is in the passive construction.

61 *until* followed by present perfect tense

We can't go any further until Mr Blake has had a look at it.

The speaker is looking forward to a time after Mr Blake's inspection of the draft (Episode 20). At this time, she will say:

Mr Blake has seen the draft. Now we can type it.

62 Omission of relative *that* before an object clause

I hope (that) he didn't find any typing errors in the ones (that) I did!

When *that* relates to an object noun or clause, as in the example above, it can be omitted. It cannot, however, be omitted when it refers to the subject.

The book that is on the desk belongs to my secretary. However, in everyday speech both *that* and the verb are usually omitted, and we say *The book on the desk belongs to my secretary*.

63 *ought*

This defective verb has only one form and can be used, like *should*, to express obligation.

The overseas people ought to (=should) speak foreign languages.

Note that *to* must always be used with *ought* but is not needed with *should*.

The negative is *ought not* (oughtn't) and the interrogative is formed by inversion:

You oughtn't to smoke so much.
Ought I to telephone the printers this morning?

64 The double genitive

This construction places emphasis on the possessor rather than the thing possessed, and is very common in spoken English.

A friend of mine works for Discovery Engineering.
Those case studies of Frank's were real teasers!

It is formed by a combination of the possessive based on *of* (for example, the house of my brother) and the possessive based on *'s* or the corresponding possessive pronoun.

The possessive pronouns are: Mine   (my)
                               Yours   (your)
                               His   (his)
                               Hers*   (her)
                               Ours   (our)
                               Theirs (their)

*The form *its* (its) is seldom, if ever used in this construction.

The double genitive is thus reached by the following stages:
    One of the friends of my brother
    One of my brother's friends
    A friend of my brother's (a friend of his)

    One of the new products of Discovery Engineering
    One of Discovery Engineering's new products
    A new product of Discovery Engineering's
    A new product of theirs

65   *either . . . or* and *neither . . . nor*

When *either . . . or* follows a negative statement, it considers the possibilities separately and indicates that they do not exist or apply:
    We do not have either the production capacity or the sales organization.

The same idea can also be expressed by *neither . . . nor* after an affirmative statement:
    We have neither the production capacity nor the sales organization.

Either form can be used in spoken English, but *neither . . . nor* is preferable in written English.

66   *used to* +infinitive

This construction indicates a state of affairs in the past which no longer applies:
    We used to have a maintenance agreement (but we no longer have one)

Do not confuse this with *to be used to* +a noun or gerund, meaning *to be accustomed to*:
    We are used to dealing with difficult problems.